First Church
of Tupelo

God Bless us
Bro. [signature]

Watch for other titles from

Running Angel Books and

Bro. Vance Moore

at

www.secondwindpublishing.com

Critical Presence: It's a God Thang

The Flood of Changed Lives at Westside Mission Center in the Aftermath of Hurricane Katrina

By

Bro. Vance Moore

Running Angel Books
Published by Second Wind Publishing, LLC.
Kernersville

Running Angel Books
Second Wind Publishing, LLC
931-B South Main Street, Box 145
Kernersville, NC 27284

First Running Angel Books edition published October 2010.
Running Angel Books, Running Angel logo, and all
production design are trademarks of Second Wind
Publishing, used under license.

For information regarding bulk purchases of this book,
digital purchase and special discounts, please contact the
publisher at www.secondwindpublishing.com

Cover design by Tracy Beltran

Manufactured in the United States of America

ISBN 978-1-935171-56-0

This book is dedicated to Jeannie, to the volunteers of the Westside Mission Center, to the people of the Great River Region and to the citizens of New Orleans with whom I experienced critical presence.

CAUTION

This is a dangerous book. This volume contains a multitude of true stories about ordinary people whose lives have been permanently, positively transformed because someone ministered to them at their moment of deepest need—or because they were the people who ministered to others at the moment of deepest need. There is a name for that experience. When a person is in profound need and someone reaches out in Christian love to render aid expecting nothing in return, it is called *critical presence*. This book tells the story of Westside Mission Center: the people who created it, who volunteer through it, who receive help from it and who on account of it have experienced spiritual transformation at a moment of critical presence. It's also a manual that explains how the experience of critical presence can be carried forward by Christians in their own lives, congregations and communities.

This book was not written to boast about the serendipity and miracles it reports. After all, these events are actually the work of God's hand. The miraculous events recorded here, as we called them at Westside, are *God Thangs*—works of the Spirit—about which no one can boast. Neither was it written simply to tell the stories of all the astonishing things that happened in the five years of Westside's outreach to the New Orleans community, of all the lives that were changed, of all the people who were transformed by the love of Christ. To be candid, too many God Thangs happened at Westside to be recorded here. Ultimately, the purpose of this book is to share how you, your church and your community can be transformed in the very same way.

Heed this caution: if you are content in your spiritual life and do not want to risk experiencing the transforming power of Christ, then do not read this book. Do not practice the principles discussed in these pages or follow the procedures explained in the final chapter. Disregard the stories, explanations, testimonials and demonstrations contained here. Otherwise, you too may open the door to the Spirit of God and ultimately find yourself transformed, empowered and swept away in the flood of God's will for your life.

Vance Moore
October 2010

Chapter 1

On the morning of January 12, 2006, my wife Jeannie and I had a special prayer. She was a patient at Baptist Hospital in North Little Rock, Arkansas, and was about to undergo surgery to have a lung removed. This was, as I recall, her sixth major surgery after having been diagnosed with breast cancer.

While we were not at all certain Jeannie would live through the procedure, her prayer that day really centered on what the two of us were going to do if she did survive. How distinctly I remember her petition to God.

"If I make it through this surgery," she prayed, "give us a mission to go to." After we had concluded our prayers, her statement to me was, "If I come through this, we have got to go and do ministry."

She didn't specifically say anything about New Orleans right then, although we had been thinking about the tragedy that had taken place there for weeks. Less than five months prior to that day, Hurricane Katrina had devastated the Gulf Coast and destroyed great portions of the Crescent City. In her prayer, Jeannie didn't mention the hurricane and the great need that resulted from the destruction. She simply repeated, "We've got to go do ministry."

Actually, Jeannie and I were already doing ministry and had been for more than a decade. I had lived out a career in the corporate world at several different levels. Toward the end of my secular career, I had been blessed to have a really good position. In my heart, however, I realized something was missing. I knew that I was being called to the ministry. Indeed, I had known for many, many years that God was calling me. Frankly, I had said "no" to the ministry for a long time.

In the early 90, I was in the field of commercial education. I was traveling quite a bit and enjoying a lot of success giving seminars and workshops. We had moved to the Little Rock area so Jeannie could be with her sister who had contracted lymphoma. Ironically, as I write this twenty years later, her sister is still with us and is lymphoma free. Then on May 4, 1996, not long after we moved to Little Rock, Jeannie found out she had cancer.

By that time, we had become very active members of the First Christian Church, Disciples of Christ, in Sherwood, Arkansas. I had been named chairman of the elders. Partly in response to the call I felt to be in ministry, we were doing workshops all across the state. On weekends when I wasn't involved in secular work, we would travel around Arkansas and conduct a little workshop we called "People of the Chalice." It was based on the book about our denominational identity written by the late Disciples clergyman Colbert S. Cartwright. Jeannie and I would go to church on Sunday morning and fulfill our responsibilities there. Then on Sunday afternoon, we would travel to another church somewhere in the state and present the workshop.

During this time, my feeling of being called to the ministry was just growing greater and greater and greater. Together Jeannie and I made a decision that, some day after I had retired, we were going to do full time ministry. Then came the discovery of her breast cancer. We gained a lot of insights and understandings as a result of that diagnosis. One thing we took from it was the prophetic realization that one never knows how much time one has in this life.

I felt that God was saying to me, "Don't wait. Don't wait. You need to do what I've called you to do. You've said 'no,' and you've said 'no' and you've said 'no.' Once again I'm confronting you and telling you that it's time to do this."

Jeannie and I talked, and together we made the decision that we would go into the ministry. She was going to be my support and I was going to be a pastor.

The beginning of our ministerial career was a bi-vocational pastorate that, in the coincidental manner that I came to associate with the hand of God, simply fell into place for us in Maumelle, Arkansas. Actually, I physically built the church in Maumelle. The congregation had gotten somewhat bogged down in its building program. Barb Jones, the regional minister of what was then the Arkansas region, asked me if I would finish the construction. During that process, the pastor of the church accepted a call to another state. The congregation called me to be the part time pastor. I physically oversaw the contractors who were building the facility while I was pastoring the church.

That ministry continued for about eighteen months until I accepted another bi-vocational call. This second one was in Jonesboro, Arkansas. Our home was still in Sherwood, so Jeannie and I traveled from Little Rock to Jonesboro for a year-and-a-half. We'd go up on Wednesday, leaving about 4 o'clock in the morning and arriving by 6:30 or 7. Then we would come home that night. On Sunday morning, we repeated the process. We maintained that bi-vocational pastorate until I received the call to become a full time pastor in Benton, Arkansas. We were still working in Benton when Hurricane Katrina hit.

At the time of Katrina, I had been at Benton for about three-and-a-half years. Jeannie and I discussed the hurricane and the damage it caused at great length. We talked about the calling I felt to go down to the Gulf Coast area and use my abilities both as a builder and as a pastor. As I'm famous for doing—until God gets my attention—I continued to say "no" to this powerful call. I refused in part because I was the caretaker for Jeannie, who by that time had endured four or five major operations already. I just didn't believe I could handle going down to the devastated area and being part of the rebuild effort while at the same time caring for my wife.

Still, as difficult as it is to acknowledge, the ministry we were doing in Benton wasn't enough for me. There comes a point—and I believe this is an experience I share with many people who have been summoned by God—when you look at your ministry, your work, and you say to yourself, "I'm fulfilling my call. I'm a pastor. I preach on Sunday morning. I visit people in the hospital. I do the things that pastors normally do." Then you sit down in your chair in your study—when it's just you and the Lord—and you confess, "It is not enough." Something was missing.

And that brings us back to the pivotal day of January 12, 2006. Jeannie did survive the operation. My regional minister, Barb Jones, had come down to be with us during the surgery. She and I sat in the waiting room after we got the good news about Jeannie and we discussed my ministry. Specifically, we discussed Jeannie's prayer and the call I was feeling to go to the disaster area as a pastor and a builder. I had a sense already that a "God Thang" was brewing. I could feel God's blessing in Jeannie's survival of that last surgery. In my heart, I knew God had heard her prayer, so I needed to listen carefully to hear God's answer.

During the course of our conversation, I began to

learn that Disciples on the local, regional and general levels were already reaching out, were already trying to find ways to create a mission site in New Orleans. On the Sunday, September 3, 2005, immediately after the hurricane made landfall, the Rev. Dr. Michael Elmore, who is a regional pastor in Baton Rouge, Louisiana, traveled to Mississippi. There he participated in worship in a Disciples church. He found first hand that Christians folks who were members of Disciples congregations in that area wanted to know how they could reach out to those who were displaced and in need. Michael wrote about the experience in a pastoral epistle:

> Today I worshipped with our congregation in McComb, Mississippi, a small church filled with loving, caring people. They cried. They sang hymns of hope. Their minister spoke of the fear and grief the disciples felt when Jesus told them he was leaving them and he would die—a grief much like what we are feeling today. But he also spoke of Jesus' words that a time was coming when his joy would fill them with a joy the world could not take away. These were words of hope I needed to hear. Before I left this church, that had also suffered from Katrina, [the members] gave me monies to help their sister churches in Louisiana and Mississippi.

He soon realized the donation from local church members in McComb was just the beginning of the help that Disciples intended to give. Here he describes some of the key Disciples leaders who became involved with assistance in the relief and rebuilding efforts soon after the disaster:

[After Katrina hit] it was several weeks before we could get into the area. Barb Jones and I and another minister at First Christian Church, Greater New Orleans, made a tour of our churches in New Orleans to assess the damage. . . . Sometime later, Jim Powell of Church Extension came to visit some of our churches. . . . Barb and I went with him to Slidell and Westside to meet with some of the members. It was following that visit the idea of a mission on the west bank was birthed.

As for me, my involvement with a mission center in New Orleans unofficially began about five hours after Jeannie's prayer as I sat with Barb in the surgical waiting room. During our discussion, both the dire situation and the great potential of Westside Christian Church came to the fore. At that moment, Westside was a small congregation located in the Algiers, Louisiana, a suburb bordering New Orleans on the west bank of the Mississippi River.

Michael Elmore, who was familiar with the congregation and had seen the church facility just a few weeks after the flood, described it: "Before Katrina, Westside was . . . down to around ten people. . . . [After the hurricane, the building] while not flooded, had sustained great damage. The roof had blown off. Mold was all around. A large tree on the property had fallen down." It was clear that this little church was going to have to be rebuilt physically, numerically and spiritually. The idea of turning it into a mission center as part of that process was already being discussed.

Barb began to tell me the story of Westside Christian Church and how it might be an ideal place for us to use as a base of operations as mission center in the New Orleans area. As we talked, it became obvious that someone was needed to direct the mission, someone who had a combination of professional expertise not only as a pastor but also as a construction person with the ability to lead clean up and rebuilding efforts.

The Moores felt the need to respond to pleas such as this one posted on a home in the Lower Ninth Ward of New Orleans.

The Westside congregation, that officially had gotten down to about twenty members before Katrina, had been in serious discussions about its future with regional officials even before the hurricane hit. Just prior to Katrina, Westside had made the decision to continue as a viable church. By that time, it had been two years since a settled pastor served the congregation. They had been using a combination of pulpit supply and visiting pastors who would come and preach. On many occasions, they met without any minister. They would have some sort of a service and share communion. After the storm, due to people being displaced and relocating, the congregation fell to a total of about ten or twelve members.

As Jeannie continued to recuperate from the surgery in the hospital, Barb and I decided to travel down to New Orleans and speak with the congregation— basically to ask if they would let us use the property as a mission. Of course, we were not trying to give any sort of ultimatum to Westside, but it was obvious the membership had dwindled significantly. The night we met with the church there were six people, if I remember correctly, who gathered with Barb and me.

We made a joint presentation. For my part, I laid out a vision for them that we would come in and share ministry and resources they could not provide on their own. I had agreed to pastor the church for the three years without a salary. Prior to the hurricane, they had not been able to pay a minister, so I knew they certainly couldn't afford one afterwards.

Our offer meant Westside was going to have to do something churches aren't often asked to do. Essentially, they would have to let me have the facility to deal with as I pleased. This was in large measure because I was going to have to make construction decisions I did not have time to take before a committee. I was going to have to make financial decisions having to do with the property. They were going to have to trust me and allow me the latitude to make those decisions. We made them the offer that, if they would give us the freedom to do it, we would take what had been the sanctuary and convert it into a sleeping arena—a bunkhouse—for volunteers to use for a set period of time. At that point, we thought it would be three years. Then we would build a new sanctuary and administration/education wing for the church. Barb and I left them after the presentation with the understanding that they were going to pray about the significant decision we set before them.

Westside Christian Church suffered extensive damage from Hurricane Katrina.

As the members reflected on their situation and the vision we presented, I'm sure they must have considered the dire situation of their facility. The property at Westside was potentially ready to be totally torn down. During the hurricane, there was not a rising flood on their side of the river, but there was tremendous damage from the 125 mile-an-hour-wind and the rain coming into their buildings unabated. Our meeting took place more than four months after Katrina and mold was everywhere. It was just a really bad, bad situation. The congregation that remained was holding service in one room of the administration building. Pat Burke, whom I consider the matriarch of the church, was running fans during the week to keep the mold from regrowing in that one room. The rest of the building was mold infested from one end to the other. During our presentation, we were honest in our description of their circumstances.

"It's easy to recognize," I said, "not only that you're devastated, but you're devastated and you're broke."

Soon I was to discover just how true that statement was. We found out that the entire insurance payment was going to be $170,000 to $200,000. It was obvious to me, however, that Westside had sustained more than $500,000 in damage.

Of course getting Westside Christian Church to accept this arrangement was only one part of the making the vision a reality. In those beginning days, we only had a dream. We had no funds and no authority to carry out what we were hoping to do. Basically, all we had was an idea of what we wanted to accomplish over a three-year period—if we could find the resources and receive the necessary approval. From a human perspective, what we were dreaming of accomplishing was virtually impossible. We knew we could only achieve what we were dreaming with the help of God.

Westside and Bro. Vance called out for others to respond to the obvious opportunity for Christian service.

Clearly, Barb and I agreed, just paving the way for a mission was going to take hard work and a fair amount of time. On the way back to Little Rock, she gave me a potential time frame for making our vision a reality.

Barb said, "Maybe we can pull this together in six months. Even though this is something we really want—no matter how much we want to proceed— Westside Christian Church has to agree to it. Without them being willing to do it, we certainly don't want to try to force the issue. Then we've got to get some help from Week of Compassion and then the Great River Region Board has got to agree to do this."

I realized she was telling me that, if this was something I felt called to do, I had six months to get all the pieces in place. That was a sobering moment. We both acknowledged it was very unlikely that we could pull any one of those significant aspects into line, much less getting all of them to fall into place in the allotted time. Six months may seem like a long period of time, but when you're trying to get a congregation, a region and the outreach ministry of a denomination to approve something that's never been done before—and provide the funds for it—it's really a brief time period.

We immediately began working to put it together. I went back and drafted the vision we had presented to Westside: the congregation was to give us the property and let us rebuild it and use it for three years as a staging area for volunteers. The physical location, I noted, was in prime position because it was centrally located within the Katrina affected areas.

To our amazement, things began to fall into place rapidly. Within one week—not six months, but one week—Westside Christian Church had said "yes." Within that same seven days, Week of Compassion (WOC, the Disciples special fund for disaster relief) had agreed to a three-year grant. Also within that week there was an executive committee meeting of the Great River Region (by that time Arkansas, Louisiana and Mississippi had merged to become the Great River Region) in which the region agreed to endorse the vision and to support the effort to create the Westside Mission Center. It is a tremendous understatement to say we were astounded. This threefold approval of the congregation, region and denomination simply underscored our conviction that God was behind us and with us and guiding us. This was a God Thang to be sure.

The situation had seemed so very bleak. We began to realize, however, that with help from WOC, the region and the multitude of the volunteers we hoped to bring in, we really might be able to rebuild Westside Christian Church and create the Westside Mission

Center. It was breathtaking to realize how astonishingly quickly everything fell into place. One significant question, however, remained—a very personal one.

On that drive back to Little Rock, Barb had said, "The final piece is that you and Jeannie are going to have to make the decision. Is this honestly what you want to do?" She was bringing up the very issue that had long prevented me from seriously considering mission work: Jeannie's recovery from surgery and ongoing health concerns.

During our meeting with the Westside congregation, I had been questioned about this from some of the people in the church. "Do you want to bring your wife down here, knowing she has cancer and that our medical facilities in New Orleans are skimpy at best right now?"

One person made the very direct statement, "You know, you could bring your wife down here and she could die."

I went back and I shared that with Jeannie and she said to me, "I am going to die somewhere anyway. Why not die doing mission?"

And that was the final piece for me, the thing that said, "We're going to go do this!" So it all came together and Jeannie and I came down to New Orleans.

Jeannie, seated with scarf, and Vance celebrate life and mission with their friends, the Kentucky Six.

Sometimes I'm asked, "What was the first God Thang that happened at Westside?" To me, the God Thangs began with Jeannie's prayer before her surgery and they have just continued in abundance ever since. Perhaps the biggest and most amazing God Thang was the way everything fell into place miraculously in such a brief period of time so Jeannie and I could come down to Westside and begin work on the church and mission.

Chapter 2

What did we encounter when we arrived in New Orleans?

To grasp the circumstances of New Orleans in the spring of 2006, it's important to reflect on the magnitude, the enormity of Hurricane Katrina. There are several standards by which hurricanes can be measured and Katrina was huge in every one of them. It's also important to know what happened—that is, to grasp the series of events that transpired—as Katrina and then Hurricane Rita roared through the Gulf Coast. And it's very important to have a basic understanding of the extent and the type of destruction that resulted. The aftermath of these storms, according to former Homeland Security Secretary Michael Chertoff, was the "worst catastrophe or set of catastrophes" in our nation's history.

In the wake of this 2005 disaster, a great deal was written very quickly: governmental reports, scholarly studies, expert opinions and personal reminiscences of people who lived through it. Despite all that's been written already, there is still much debate, controversy and disagreement about precisely what did happen, why it happened and how it can be prevented from happening again in the future. In fact, it is still quite unclear exactly what the long-term effects of the disaster will be economically, environmentally and culturally.

It's far beyond the scope of this book—and a distraction from my intended purpose—to try to address these big issues about Katrina and the storm's ultimate impact. However, it's important to give an overview of the events and to discuss a few basic facts about the disaster because of their effects on Westside Mission Center and our rebuilding efforts. As a disclaimer, let me warn you that you may find it disturbing to read the descriptions of the storm, its aftermath and the resulting human suffering. Thus, I encourage you to be sure to read the "miracle parts" that follow—the many accounts of "God Thangs" in subsequent chapters.

For years prior to Hurricane Katrina, climatologists had been predicting a cyclic upswing in annual hurricanes and their intensity. This prediction was proving accurate even before 2005, which turned out to be the most active hurricane season in recorded history. The 2005 hurricane season set a great many ominous records, among which are the total number of tropical depressions (thirty-one), total number of named storms (twenty-eight), total number of hurricanes (fifteen), number of Category 5 hurricanes in one year (four), the highest sustained wind speed (Hurricane Wilma, 185 mph), the total amount of damage from hurricanes ($144 billion), and finally the greatest length of season (with Tropical Storm Arlene forming June 8 and Tropical Storm Zeta ending on January 6, 2006).

As I mentioned above, there are various ways of measuring hurricanes. Most of us are familiar with what is called the Saffir-Simpson Hurricane Scale that primarily uses sustained wind speed to categorize storms on a scale of 1-5. Hurricanes are also measured geographically, according to how far out hurricane or tropical storm force winds extend from their center. These storms are also evaluated by barometric pressure: typically the lower the pressure, the more intense the storm. Then there is a factor called "accumulated cyclone energy" (ACE), that is the strength of a hurricane multiplied by the length of time it exists.

Considering the ultimate impact of Katrina, while by every standard it was an enormous storm, it was neither the largest nor most intense of the 2005 hurricane season. The unenviable record Katrina did set is destruction. Various estimates set the total damages caused by Hurricane Katrina at from $80 billion to $100 billion dollars, and the estimate of the damages is still continuing to grow. The total damages caused by all hurricanes in 2005 was an estimated $144 billion. Thus, even though it was only one of five major storms to cause significant damage in the United States that year, Katrina was responsible for about two thirds of the total destruction.

A collapsed public school building in the Lower Ninth Ward, untouched two years after the storm.

By way of giving a more tangible illustration, Louisiana journalist Jamie Colby wrote that, if the total amount of debris created by Katrina (118 million cubic yards) were placed in an area the size of a football field, the mound of trash would be ten-and-a-half miles high. By contrast, the next most destructive storm on record, Hurricane Andrew in 1992, caused only about one-sixth as much damage as Katrina.

The storm began as a tropical depression near the Bahamas on August 23 and moved north and west toward the southern tip of Florida. By the time it made landfall in between Hallandale Beach and Adventura, Florida, on August 25, it had barely achieved Category 1 hurricane status. Nevertheless, it created massive damage and ultimately caused fourteen deaths in the state. Crossing South Florida, Katrina began a south-to-north arc through the Gulf of Mexico, the warm waters of which were conducive to strengthening the storm's intensity. On August 27, Katrina attained Category 3 designation, meaning sustained winds of more than 110 mph.

Soon afterward, the hurricane experienced a phenomenon called an "eyewall replacement cycle." This event, which is a characteristic of very intense hurricanes, occurs when the well-defined "eye" in the center of the storm breaks down and another eye forms. In such cases, the storm loses intensity, but expands geographically. The result of this particular replacement cycle was the doubling in size of Katrina to a diameter of about 240 miles. The loss of intensity was short-lived, as the hurricane quickly regained Category 3 status. Then, over the course of nine hours, it went from Category 3 to Category 5. By 1 p.m. on August 28, Katrina achieved maximum sustained winds of 175 mph and a barometric pressure of 26.64. This made Katrina the fourth largest Atlantic hurricane and the strongest hurricane ever in the Gulf of Mexico. It possessed the lowest barometric pressure ever recorded (although within a few weeks both Hurricanes Rita and Wilma would surpass each of these records). About 6 a.m. the next morning, Katrina made landfall at Buras-Triumph, Louisiana, sixty-five miles southeast of New Orleans. It was then a Category 3 hurricane with sustained winds of 125 mph and with hurricane force winds extending out 120 miles from its center. The storm followed a north-northeast path, continuing to maintain hurricane force winds as it crossed over Meridian, Mississippi. Katrina was not downgraded from tropical storm status until it passed over Clarksville, Tennessee. Its remnants moved north and east, affecting the Great Lakes area and finally eastern Canada.

As the threat of Katrina had grown, evacuations had occurred all along the areas that might potentially be impacted. In Florida, hurricane warnings were posted more than twenty-four hours before landfall and a voluntary evacuation was advised by the state. The intensifying hurricane drew the attention of Gulf Coast authorities, especially after the initial damage it caused in South Florida. The projected path of the storm at first was for a landfall along the Alabama-Florida coastal area. The vast size of Katrina caused the warning area to be extended to the Mississippi and Louisiana's coastal areas on August 25 as well. That same day a federal state of emergency was declared that included portions of Louisiana.

In the following days, the continued steady northerly movement of Katrina toward Louisiana eventually pushed the projected landfall point closer to New Orleans. The official forecast predicted a 29% possibility of a direct hit on the Crescent City. On August 28, less than twenty-four hours before landfall, a mandatory evacuation of New Orleans and large areas of southeast Louisiana was ordered. From Alabama to Louisiana, more than 1,000,000 people were told to relocate out of the reach of the storm.

Beyond the natural fears of citizens in the hurricane's path, local leaders and government officials were extremely concerned about the potential destruction a major hurricane might cause in New Orleans. Prior to Katrina's landfall, Max Mayfield, the Director of the National Hurricane Center, warned White House administrators that the projected storm surge (the seawater tide that accompanies hurricanes) could conceivably exceed the height of New Orleans' levees.

Warnings about the possible dire results of a major hurricane hitting the New Orleans area were well known and had been documented for more than forty years. In the aftermath of Katrina, Mayor Ray Nagin was quoted as saying, "This was the storm we have been afraid of for years."

Despite the advanced warnings and great intensity of Katrina, evacuations proceeded slowly. The state of Louisiana had previously created an orderly, three-phase evacuation plan that would have given thirty hours for the total evacuation of the New Orleans area. A mandatory evacuation of New Orleans itself, however, was not ordered until nineteen hours prior to Katrina's landfall. It has been suggested that the sudden crush of people trying to get out of the area overwhelmed the transportation infrastructure.

Compounding the situation was the mounting damage Katrina was causing to the transportation arteries. Eventually there were only two routes out of the city, both leading west. There were impassable gaps in eastbound I-10. Rail traffic via Amtrak came to a standstill. Though the Louis Armstrong International

Airport north of the city did not flood, it closed to air traffic before Katrina's landfall and remained closed to passenger travel until September 13, two weeks after the storm.

By some estimates, 60,000 New Orleans citizens had not been evacuated by the time Katrina made landfall. Anecdotally I've heard that many old-time residents had endured hurricanes and floods in New Orleans before and elected to stay and ride out the hurricane. Many believed that, as with previous storms, the water wouldn't rise higher than a few feet. In the Lower Ninth Ward even today it's obvious that pre-Katrina homes were often built two or three feet off the ground in anticipation of floods similar to what residents had experienced in the past. It has also been said that recovery workers after the storm sometimes found the bodies of residents in the upper portions of their attics, where they had continued to move higher up in hopes that the flood waters would stop rising.

Those who remained in New Orleans at the time of Katrina's landfall found few sources of safe, high ground. Much media attention in the days following the storm was focused on the Superdome athletic stadium. City officials had anticipated that virtually all residents would get out safely before Katrina hit. The Superdome was announced to be the "refuge of last resort" for the few who might not make it out. It had been supplied with food and necessities intended to accommodate up to 800 people for several days. In the days following Katrina, 26,000 people sought refuge in the Superdome.

A second, completely unintended "refuge of last resort" was the Ernest N. Morial Convention Center. Residents still seeking evacuation on August 29 began to arrive at the convention center, where buses were supposed to provide transportation out of the city. By the next morning, a crowd of about 1000 people had arrived, but there were no transports. At some point, the convention center was broken into and occupied. Before it was evacuated on September 4, up to 20,000 people sought shelter there, despite the absence of food, safe water or other necessities.

For several hours after Katrina's landfall, the New Orleans area was subjected to sustained, straight winds of 75 to 125 mph. The amount of rainfall during the storm averaged eight to ten inches. Along with the rain, a storm surge of from twelve to twenty-seven feet of water moved inland through the canals, channels and rivers that permeate the New Orleans area. Sitting just to the north and east of New Orleans, Lake Ponchartrain, the second largest saltwater lake in the United States, also experienced this surge.

The result of this rapidly accumulated water with accompanying high winds is called "SLOSH" (Sea, Lake and Overland Surges from Hurricanes): the fresh water present in rivers, reservoirs and lakes around the affected geographical area becomes part of a hurricane's destructive power. Hurricane Katrina has become the textbook example of SLOSH. The federal agency NOAA (National Oceanic and Atmospheric Administration) predicted with reasonable accuracy the extent of surging water the affected area was going to experience a full twenty-four hours before the hurricane's landfall.

Ultimately, the SLOSH surge coursing through New Orleans's waterways was both slightly less than NOAA had predicted and somewhat less than the amount the canals, levees and floodwalls were designed to withstand. As has repeatedly been stated, the flood system of New Orleans was built to handle a Category

3 hurricane and Katrina was a Category 3 hurricane when it struck the city. The flood system, however, failed disastrously. In the words of a report given two years after the storm by the American Society of Civil Engineers, the flooding of New Orleans by Hurricane Katrina was "the worst engineering catastrophe in American History."

All in all, storm water broke through floodwalls, levees and canals in fifty-three different locations, inundating 80% of the city and 100% of Saint Bernard Parish on the eastern side of New Orleans. The Mississippi River Gulf Outlet (commonly called "Mr. Go"), a long canal built in the 1960's to provide swift access to the Mississippi River north of New Orleans, was breeched by floodwater in twenty places. Additionally, the funnel-like design of Mr. Go resulted in the SLOSH water from Lake Ponchartrain picking up speed as it flowed into the unprotected, low-lying areas of the city, much the way a nozzle on a water hose condenses its flow and thus intensifies its force.

Pumping stations were in place throughout the area for the purpose of reducing water levels in the canal system. Within eleven hours of Katrina's landfall, all pumps had failed. Therefore, since large portions of the city were below sea level and there was no active or passive mechanism through which they could retreat, the floodwaters remained standing throughout the city for days. On September 23, twenty-five days after Katrina hit, Hurricane Rita's SLOSH surge flooded portions of New Orleans again, flowing through the already existing canal and levee openings into areas like the Lower Ninth Ward.

When the floodwater at last retreated, the destruction was massive. Of the 300,000 homes destroyed by Katrina, 100,000 were in the New Orleans area. Prior to the storm, there were approximately 455,000 residents of greater New Orleans. In the aftermath of Katrina, about 250,000 people departed in search of housing and work.

Of course, New Orleans was not the only area in the Gulf Coast region to experience depopulation. It's estimated that between 800,000 and 1,000,000 people relocated immediately following the storm—the largest dispersion of Americans since the Great Depression. A great many abandoned all their possessions, legal documents, keepsakes and pets (roughly 600,000 cats and dogs were killed or abandoned as a result of Katrina). These sudden, irreversible moves made it extremely difficult for family members to contact one another, and thus for officials to determine how many people had died and how many had relocated.

A typical spray painted door in the Lower Ninth Ward after Hurricane Katrina, indicating the date of house's inspection and what was found.

Michael Elmore's essay, "Reflections From Baton Rouge After Katrina," was written less than a week after Katrina's landfall and does a great job of capturing the immediate reactions and experience in the affected area:

I do not remember a time that I have been so anxious, so emotionally drained, so spiritually exhausted and this is just the beginning. All around are people suffering, scared, uncertain about their future. Chaos is everywhere I look. How can this be? Will this ever end?

The largest city in Louisiana is now Baton Rouge. One fourth of the population of Louisiana has been displaced and most have been relocated across the country as far away as Portland, OR. Our state will never be the same, hopefully it will be better, but never the same. All our lives have been changed, never to be the same. I go to sleep every night listening to helicopters flying from New Orleans and the Gulf Coast and arise every morning to the same sound. I wait in gas lines and go to a McDonald's that will only serve through the drive-through window because fights have broken out in their dining room. Not by people from New Orleans, but by local troublemakers taking advantage of a terrible situation. I visit our church in McComb, Mississippi where the town has a 7:00 pm curfew.

Baton Rouge has doubled in size. So has Shreveport. Lafayette has a Cajun Dome filled with people. Leesville has opened shelters as have sister states in Mississippi and Texas, Alabama, Arkansas and others. Churches and individuals have opened their doors and are

*housing and feeding thousands of people.
People across our nation and around the world
are responding to the terrible tragedy and the
human need in Louisiana, Mississippi and
Alabama.*

*Now is not the time to blame or point
fingers, now is the time for God's people to join
hearts and hands and feed the hungry, clothed
the naked, care for the sick, house the homeless,
give drink to the thirsty. There is enough work
of compassion to keep us all busy.*

One good way to grasp what was happening all
along the Gulf Coast is to hear the reports of those who
first stepped forward to help. Tom Sikes, Pastor of
First Christian in Meridian, Mississippi, pooled a
medical team within hours of Katrina's landfall. His
descriptions of what the team encountered are stunning
and heartrending:

*When we bounded from our cars, in shock
and awe at the destruction, we were met by a
single, solitary nurse who was overwhelmed
with the need. She was serving at Trinity
Episcopal School in Long Beach and that is
where we found our call. On this road in
between antebellum history and complete
devastation, God was calling this group of first
responders to help this lone nurse. We set up a
medical clinic and began helping her with
medicines, pharmaceuticals, cleanup, food and
prayer.*

*I was stationed in this section to offer
pastoral care alongside nurses and doctors.
What I saw was a pattern of pain. The first*

station was seeking basic information of each patient. I saw the very poor alongside the very rich. The classes merged through this storm. I saw fishing boat captains dressed in their fishing shirts alongside children who had no shirts. All were equal and seeking medical care. At the first station, the people seemed stoic. At the second station of triage, they remained calm. But something happened when they finally saw a doctor. Each of them seemed to release their emotions. I saw tears, heard the cries, and felt the pain of these survivors. A bond began to form as medicine became the platform for providing God's critical presence.

One particular lady received medical and pastoral care. She wanted to give back. Three hours later, without a kitchen in her own home, she found another and returned with fresh gumbo for us. She just wanted to say thank you with action!

Ultimately, it was estimated that 1836 people died as a result of Hurricane Katrina. The largest percentage of these was in Louisiana, which lost 1577 citizens. There are still approximately 135 individuals from the state who disappeared during the storm and its aftermath and whose fates are unknown.

This New Orleans monument remembers the citizens of New Orleans who perished in Hurricanes Katrina and Rita.

Many people who did not live in the area were still profoundly affected because they had family and close friends who were impacted—or who might have been impacted. Not knowing about the situation and the welfare of loved ones created an atmosphere of crisis for those who were nowhere near the storm. Alex Watkins, who was at the time a student in the University of Mississippi in Oxford, describes this situation quite well:

> *I remember watching the coverage unfold on television and seeing the devastation that was taking place not only in New Orleans but also along the coast. I remember seeing friends, classmates, teachers, leaving school because they could not get into contact with their families after the storm. I specifically remember hearing one of my friends tell me that his home*

was completely destroyed but his family was safe because they had evacuated Bay St. Louis, Mississippi, to family in a different area.

Death and dispersion were just the beginning of troubles facing those who wished to return to their homes in New Orleans. Assistance from governmental agencies and first-response non-governmental organizations was unreliable and unevenly distributed. In the eventual investigation conducted by the US Congress, it was officially reported that, "FEMA (the Federal Emergency Management Agency) and the Red Cross did not have a logistics capacity sophisticated enough to fully support the massive number of Gulf Coast victims." In other words, the disaster was so great that neither the government nor helpful organizations could cope with it.

Many residents lived for unexpectedly long periods in FEMA trailers.

Along with residents, businesses also left the Crescent City. Security became an overriding issue. The national media reported frequently on murders, looting, carjackings, rapes and robberies. As it turned out, much of what was reported was inaccurate, but ultimately almost 47,000 federal troops and National Guard members were sent to restore order.

A toxic environment was another significant issue faced by the returning population. The combination of pollutants spread by the floodwater included: gasoline and oil, lead, arsenic and *E. coli* (the deadly bacteria that grows in human and animal waste). Particularly dangerous were the multitudes of various mold infestations present everywhere. As a result of these toxic conditions, health care officials began to encounter mold related asthma, oral sores, septic infections, tetanus, Hepatitis and a multitude of other infections.

Those trying to rebuild their homes faced daunting obstacles. For example, a typical situation was that the owner of a residence in New Orleans would have a mortgage against his or her dwelling and the home had been rendered uninhabitable by the hurricane. In this situation, the homeowner's insurance company would issue a check for the appraised value of the home made out to the mortgage company—the actual legal owner of the home. The loan company or bank would then issue a check for any remaining equity, the money remaining after the loan balance was paid, and send it along with the title to the homeowner. In most cases, the equity payment would be much less than the replacement cost of the house. The mortgage company, however, would typically refuse to make another loan since the property was obviously in a potential flood area. So the homeowner held a deed to a mold-infested, unlivable, condemned house along with an equity check that was far too small to pay the cost of rebuilding.

Having lost all their possessions, homeowners also often lost control of the fate of their homes after the hurricane.

A second scourge that confronted many who wanted to rebuild was contractor fraud. Reputable contractors were overwhelmed with more work than they could do. Those who wanted to utilize their services were forced to wait for months or years. In the face of this lack of qualified builders, a number of individuals appeared who represented themselves to be contractors. Often they would gain the confidence of a homeowner and get that person to turn over to them whatever funds were available for the reconstruction of their homes. Little or no actual work was done and the fraudulent contractor would simply move on to other victims. Thus, many residents lost their homes, their possessions, their jobs, their ability to borrow funds and ultimately the insurance money they received for their losses.

A direct result of this common chain of events was an attitude of distrust toward strangers who offered assistance. As you'll read in Chapter 5, when I first asked Pastor Howard Washington if I could help him rebuild the Greater New Jerusalem Missionary Baptist Church, his automatic response was, "I told you, I ain't got no money." Another person who had a difficult time accepting the help of strangers was Thelma Tyler, who sat outside her house for days watching as we rebuilt Dee Jones' home, two doors down from hers. At last she approached me one day to announce that she finally decided she could trust me and she was ready for the Westside volunteers to fix her house.

It is important, I think, to step aside from the statistics and reports and simple magnitude of the disaster. To really understand the aftermath of the storm, it must be seen from a human viewpoint, as above where I described my first conversation with Pastor Washington. To understand the real tragedy and the real suffering, you have to encounter the people who endured the disaster.

Michael Elmore not only ministered to but also closely observed the people of the Gulf Coast area as they tried to rebuild their lives after the storm. I was struck by one of his comments about the permanent changes in their attitudes. He said:

> *I heard someone talk about what they called the 'Katrina Effect.' They said they have a box filled with photos, valuables and so forth that they do not want to lose. They keep it in an easily accessible place where they can pick it up quickly in the event they need to evacuate. So*

there has been a clear, lasting impact on the mindset of those who went through Katrina.

Another person whose life was completely changed by the hurricane was Gwen Till. I met her several years after the storm, and after we had rebuilt Westside Christian Church. As the congregation began to grow, she came to worship there with some of her friends and I learned her story.

Gwen had been a resident of the New Orleans area for forty-five years prior to Katrina. Three generations of her family lived in the region. In describing the experience of August 29, 2005, she wrote:

I left Sunday, the day before the storm made landfall. It hit on Monday. Everyone left. That's just what you're supposed to do in a case like that. I had always left when the storms came in. You know to take three days worth of things: clothes and stuff like that you know you'll need. I left New Orleans thinking I'd be back in three days. That's the way it had always been.

I went east to D'lo, Mississippi. They tell you not to go east because that's the direction the storm is going to go, but I went east anyway because I have a sister inland. We did experience some of the storm there. The rest of my family went to Texas to stay with my brother. He had a full house—nine adults and four dogs.

Very quickly, I found out things were not going to be the way they had been before. You couldn't come home not just for three days, but for three weeks. They began to let people come back by sections and you had to get your shots before you could come back. You had to show proof of your vaccinations. You had to have your driver's license to get in. Policemen were at every section checking people's licenses.

Well, the house was there all right. There had been water all the way to the ceilings: ten feet of water and there was mud twelve inches high. I couldn't open the front door because it had a couch up against it. I couldn't open the back door because it had a refrigerator up against it. I tried and tried, but I couldn't get in. Finally, on the fourth day I made up my mind I was going to get in. Somehow, I pushed hard enough on the front door to move the couch and I got it open.

Somebody asked me if I was emotionally prepared for what I found. Not really. You start to prepare for the 160-mile drive to your house. You see all the other homes and you start thinking about it. You emotionally cannot be prepared for that: to see that everything you owned had floated and landed somewhere else where it wasn't supposed to be. You walked over things that had floated all around your house. It was scary at times.

Afterwards I decided to live in Mississippi. I had lost everything in New Orleans. Eighty percent of the people were gone. I was very lucky. I was able to take retirement. I was a hairdresser. Yes, getting out was the right decision for me. I could see God everywhere, it seemed. He just sent me where I was supposed to be. It helped that I do have family in New Orleans, so I was able to go back and forth. And I wasn't stranded like so many people.

That helped with my healing.
I had a girlfriend. She and her family were
still living in New Orleans. I would go visit her.
I stayed with her when I came to the city. She
and her boyfriend went to Westside Christian
Church and I started going with them as well.

In the face of the horrendous natural disaster of Katrina and the failures of so many governmental and social institutions to bring timely and necessary assistance, it is inspiring to see the resilience of the many citizens of New Orleans. I'm amazed by these people who decided against all odds and in the face of all challenges to stay and rebuild. As my friend Michael Elmore has reminded me upon occasion, "Hurricane Katrina was a manmade disaster, assisted by nature." That disaster began with a terrible storm that revealed human mistakes and then human weaknesses; but ultimately what it most revealed was hope and compassion. One result of Hurricane Katrina was the bringing together of the needs of the people of New Orleans and the talents of the willing volunteers of Westside Mission Center.

Jeannie and I came to New Orleans at this moment when the needs we were going to address were at their deepest point. This prepared us to step into a world where we would experience the ministry of critical presence again and again.

Chapter 3

Jeannie remained in Arkansas the first thirty days I was in New Orleans. She was still recuperating from surgery and we had no place to live. There *were* no places to live.

We had discussions from the beginning about bringing down a travel trailer because we didn't qualify for one of the FEMA trailers. I didn't own a trailer, however, and there wasn't one to be had in New Orleans. I simply couldn't find one.

Eventually we sold our home in Sherwood, Arkansas, and took part of the proceeds to purchase a thirty-two foot trailer I found there. I brought it down and set it up on the Westside property and Jeannie and I moved in.

The original plan was for us to live in the trailer for about a month until we found a place, like a parsonage, to rent. We didn't fully think through the situation. Livable real estate was a prime need at that time. Any kind of a decent residential rental was $1500-$2000 a month and there simply weren't any available. So that one month stay turned out to be sixteen months.

After we had been in the trailer for several months, we discovered Jeannie's cancer had come back. She went on working side-by-side with me at the mission to the extent she could and all the while she was receiving treatment.

Somebody in the church picked at her one day about living in a twenty-nine foot trailer. It was thirty-two feet long, but three feet of that was the tongue; so the living space was less than twenty-nine feet. The remark was made, "You're living there with Vance and two dogs and you've been there for a pretty good while now. Isn't that a rough way to live?"

I recall as if it were yesterday Jeannie responding, "That's my mansion."

The volunteers who heard the exchange queried her about that. They said, "You know, Jeannie, we know you have a positive attitude, but a twenty-nine foot trailer is not a mansion."

She said, "Well, when it's hot, I push a button and it gets cool. When I need to go to the bathroom, I push a button and it goes away. When I need to eat, I turn a knob and the heat comes on in the oven. And I know that there are many, many people living down under the bridge on Canal Street who can't do anything of those things. Yes, I live in a mansion."

The famous travel trailer that Jeannie called her mansion.

During the time we were rebuilding Westside and Jeannie and I were living in the trailer, we realized the church was not going to be able to find suitable, affordable housing—not just for us but for whoever followed us. We weren't just thinking about our own circumstances, but more about the future of Westside Christian Church. So we approached the region and together made the decision to build a parsonage. Our intention was not to build a parsonage for two older folks, like Jeannie and me. Rather we built it in anticipation of a young family that would someday pastor Westside.

When we talk about building the parsonage, it's important to give credit to the Great River Region. The region owned a piece of property in another city and sold it. The regional board voted to appropriate $70,000 of the proceeds from that sale to help fund the building of the Westside parsonage. We took volunteer labor and $70,000 plus some other donations from material suppliers and built the parsonage. Today that home is valued at $185,000, which is median for the neighborhood around the church. It's three bedrooms, two baths—just one foot less than 2000 square feet—and it's paid for. That's another God Thang.

As for the sort of work we were doing at Westside, I saw this first as an opportunity to build a church. After all, I had come into the ministry to do evangelism and teaching. As a congregation, Westside wasn't non-existent, but it had gotten down to ten or fifteen members. Then there was the mission we wanted to start. The property itself was totally devastated and there was very little funding to rebuild it. Here was a congregation that needed pastoral ministry.

Second, here was a mission that needed a director. From the beginning our thought was that the church and the mission center were both sort of at the same place—just about as far down as you could go without going out of existence altogether. Westside Christian Church and Westside Mission Center were like that valley of skeletons the prophet Ezekiel saw. His immediate comment was, "The bones were exceedingly dry." And we heard the voice of the Lord asking, "Can these bones live again?" We knew the church and the mission would not come to life without a lot of work on behalf of a lot of volunteers, but more than that it simply wasn't going to happen without the help of God.

Vance celebrates an outdoor communion for the Westside congregation.

I've read the comments of Michael Elmore from around the time we began at Westside. They're both complimentary and reminiscent of the magnitude of the task we found ourselves facing:

> *I did not know Vance very well before he came to Westside. I had met him at a few board meetings, but we had never talked. The thing that impressed me about Vance and Jeannie was*

their passion for God and God's church and mission. Vance poured his heart and soul into not just rebuilding a facility but into a mission that grew out of all that ended up going on there. I saw him develop a deep relationship with the congregation and with the volunteers who came to be a part of the mission. None of us saw the extent of this ministry unfolding as it did. We were all surprised by God through the work he had for us to do. Westside was a "God Thang," just as Vance always said.

Tom Sikes shared with me his account of coming to Westside when we first started the work of rebuilding. It's humbling to read his words and remember those experiences:

Rev. Barb Jones invited me to a meeting at Westside Christian Church. For some reason, I brought a team of church members who had expertise in building and mission. In reflection, I am sure the others thought we were barnstorming in. But I knew that those around me were ready to serve to the fullest extent they could. They included those who had served faithfully in the other missions including Ed Owen who spearheaded the first responders as well as Rick Justice who quietly and faithfully served behind the scenes. I brought B.B. Archer, a well-known architect and elder who was ready to be used by God in the critical presence of his beloved New Orleans.

We heard the vision of Barb and Vance Moore to come to Westside Christian Church and use that church as a missional church, called by God, shaped by scripture and sent to serve those in between as well. We took a look at the facility. The walls were old and the ceilings low, yet it was dry. We saw a different context for mission here. The houses and churches were standing, unlike those we had seen along the Mississippi coast that were obliterated. Here in the Queen City, the lady fought back. Houses indeed were standing but the water and wind damage made the mission even more difficult.

Vance Moore introduced himself alongside his wife Jeannie. We discovered that they too had sensed the call to "get up and go toward the south." And they were ready to leave Arkansas, come to New Orleans, and use their gifts of ministry to reveal God's presence. They were sharing this vision and we caught it!

The room was electrified with God's Spirit as we all pulled together and began to act. Soon churches from around the country began to pour in volunteers and money.

Our task was to help with the rebuilding of the church as a mission center. We paid for a steel company from Meridian to come and build a place to sleep over 50 volunteer missionaries. We paid for 50 mattresses. Eventually we helped rebuild a parsonage so Vance and Jeannie would no longer have to live in a tiny travel trailer. Our members went on weekends alongside other churches from around the country. Together we saw—it was a God Thang.

Nightly, after long days of sweat and service, Vance fed each team and gathered the troops for a reflection time. With honesty and integrity and sincerity, he shared his story. People were astounded that he would leave safe Arkansas to come to New Orleans and help rebuild the city. But what amazed them and us most was that his wife was living with brain cancer. They had every right to say "no." to the call to "get up and go on the road in between." But they did not. And their witness of God's call and boldness to be led by the Spirit into the wilderness was so strong it carried the rest of us deeper into our commitment to humbly serve.

Vance Moore used his skills as a building contractor along with his gifts for pastoral care. He represented for many of us the Christ. A carpenter by trade and a listener like the Lord, he knelt down with children and cared. He raised his strong arms and carried sheet rock. He went to Lowe's day in and day out buying more materials, coordinating the scores of teams of volunteers, and navigating the many personalities involved with grace and grit.

Michael Elmore has also done an excellent job of describing the way our vision and our mission morphed as we began to undertake rebuilding the church and creating the mission center:

Barb brought Vance down to meet with the folks at Westside and me to share our vision for rebuilding the church literally—its building, the rebuilding of its membership and developing a mission base. As we moved into the process and as buildings were constructed, as volunteers came and recovery work grew, the mission center became the dominant focus. Gradually the focus shifted to mission and recovery while Westside Christian Church grew slowly. I think we were all surprised by the shift. I had concerns from the beginning about the growth of the church; I saw the possibility of Westside Mission Center becoming a long-term recovery center, as I knew there would be needs for years.

The initial vision we presented was to take the church and convert it to a mission center. We would use it as a mission staging area for three years, doing as much as we could. Our assumption was that, over that period as the city was restored, the amount of rebuild work in the city would decrease. In balance then, after the mission work began to conclude, we intended to spend a large block of time rebuilding the church—the numerical membership—so that the congregation would increase. We thought we'd start out with "little church-big mission" and end up with "big church-little mission."

Of course, it didn't work that way at all. As soon as we began to do mission work, the requirements on my time and energy grew more and more until the mission became a fulltime, seven-day-a-week job. I found that the demands of the rebuilding effort out in the community would only allow me to be a pastor to the church in the capacity of preaching a sermon every Sunday.

The question I'm often asked about that is whether or not the Westside congregation felt as if they were being shortchanged. Oddly enough—or perhaps miraculously enough—the answer is "no."

The church has been an important part of the mission since the beginning. That handful of members wanted to be a part of Westside Mission Center, but they had many outside responsibilities. One of them was taking care of a husband who had special needs and a mother who was elderly and also had special needs. Most of the others worked. One was over eighty-years-old. They could not go into the mission field to assist with the rebuilding.

Still they had this great desire to help. So about a year into our mission work, the people of Westside got together and made the decision they would cook meals for the volunteers once a week. They began this outreach in 2007 and they continued it as long as the mission center remained open. Every Wednesday night they fed the volunteers and spent time in fellowship with them. They did this just as a way to say "thank you" to the volunteers and as a way to stay connected to the rebuild efforts that were going on. Through all the years, they never once asked for any money to do any of that. They reached in their pockets personally and did it. They cooked the meals, they prepared the meals, they came down to the mission center to serve the meals and they visited with the volunteers.

Regarding the outlook of the Westside congregation, early on I think there was a sense of skepticism. This attitude in the congregation was not dissimilar from that of most of the people in New Orleans at that time. There was disbelief felt by residents here that people would come and give up of their time and their money with no desire other than to help them.

It was also the case that the people of Westside Christian Church had been part of a region—the Louisiana Region before it became part of the Great River Region—that had struggled with its connection to the larger church for years. Many of our small churches in Louisiana, and I think this is true in most regions, didn't feel the connection to the larger church that our larger congregations did. They didn't have the communication with the larger church, the general church. The members of small, struggling congregations like Westside very often felt as if they were out there all by themselves.

So when I met these Westside people, I encountered a certain amount of, "You say you really want to help us, but you've never been here before. So what's different now? When we needed a pastor and couldn't find one, where were you?"

Again, I think this is a perception smaller congregations have about toward the larger church. So when we came in and made the proposal, they said "yes" with a certain degree of skepticism. Later, as they saw volunteers coming in, as they saw Westside Christian Church being rebuilt, as they saw Westside Mission Center being created, and as they saw the little trailer parked out there knowing that Jeannie and I lived in it, their skepticism very quickly turned to love. Soon it was the case that volunteers would come to the mission center and the members of the congregation would come by to meet them.

For years, the members of Westside served supper to mission center volunteers.

I remember a number of afternoons when Roseanne Stubbs, a long-time faithful member of Westside, would come by and I would find her sitting out on the sidewalk. She would just sit there, talking to the volunteers, sharing her story with them. That's something that, in another setting, we might call commonplace. Only it was not at all commonplace in New Orleans following the devastation folks experienced. This was another example of critical presence: experiencing Christ by meeting people at the moment of their greatest need—though, even while I witnessed it frequently, I had no name yet for what I was seeing.

When they started doing the Wednesday evening fellowship suppers, I think it was to be supportive of me, of what we were trying to accomplish. Almost immediately that changed into the attitude: "This is what we, the church, want to do to be part of the recovery effort." I was seeing that same transforming experience I had seen in the volunteers also occurring in the members of Westside Christian Church. Over the years, I heard them tell the story of their church and their experiences many, many times. As I listened, their stories deepened in warm and wonderful spiritual ways. I know it's because God has transformed a lot of their thinking about Jesus and how he extends love to us through our interactions with other people.

I should note that, from the very beginning, the mission work they were doing not only caused volunteers to learn new skills, but brought out the best in them as giving Christians and opened them to the experience of critical presence. It also caused them to exceed all their ordinary, realistic expectations. An anecdote shared by Don Miller from Manchester, Missouri, really expresses this well:

Something else happened that totally defied logic: the "mud hens." When I went down to Westside, I did a lot of drywall taping. Vance saved those jobs for me. While we were working on the sanctuary at Westside, I told Vance I wanted that done correctly and I was going to do it. We had about thirty-four people working there on that trip. The sanctuary was ready to be taped and I was working until ten each night, but I realized I just wasn't going to have time. It was too much and it didn't take me long to realize I wasn't going to get there.

On Tuesday morning, I looked at the group of people sitting there and I asked, "How many people here know how to tape?" All the handyman types looked down to avoid eye contact. There were seven women sitting there

*who were willing to do the taping. They
included two nurses, a nutritionist, two teachers
and a lawyer. I thought, "Oh my God, you're
kidding me. I'm going to teach these women
how to tape a job that just has to be done
right." I spent an hour-and-a-half showing
them the basics.*

*They spent two days taping. I did the finish
coat. On the third day they moved into a house
and began taping there. They got the name "the
mud hens." Their children came in to help them
and learned as well and they became the "mud
chicks." Any volunteer who was shown
something and just asked to do it, could do what
they were asked. That was an eye opener for
me. The majority of those women are still very
invested in WMC.*

Berea Christian Church member Crystin Faenza
wrote me after a mission trip about this phenomenon.
She has a great way of describing what happened
constantly to Westside volunteers:

*The experience of working at Westside has
strengthened and reinforced my belief that
anything is possible with God. It amazes me to
see the amount of work that we are able to
accomplish in such a short period of time. We
start the week concerned, looking anxiously at
how much is ahead of us. We end the week
looking back at how much we were able to get
done. It also amazes me how we all find
ourselves doing things we would never have
believed we could. We all find hidden talents.*

From the outset, we faced many obstacles on many fronts. A lot of people would look at Jeannie and me and say, "How long are you going to stay in that trailer?" Our attitude about the trailer was: "This is home." Still we knew sooner or later that we would have to move out of it. The city wasn't going to let us keep the trailer on the church property and live in it forever. This helped us come to understand another challenge about living in a trailer. We learned we would have to deal with something faced by many people who, after Katrina, lived in New Orleans in FEMA trailers: the physical part of living in a trailer is not as difficult as the mental part of living in it. There is no doubt in your mind that the place you're living in is not the home you lost; you're living in a trailer. It's not a mobile home either. It's a little trailer with that hitch on the front you can't hide. And sooner or later, you begin to hear people from the city government say, "You can't stay here."

We would respond, "But I'm here trying to rebuild the city."

"You still can't stay here."

I have to say that I experienced this attitude, this dynamic, regarding more than just living in a trailer. In the beginning, we received a tremendous amount of resistance to our outreach efforts from people in the local governmental. Clearly, it was their way of saying to us, "Go away."

In a way that was absurd because we were the people they most needed and it was at the time when they needed us the most. In fairness to them, I think they were just overwhelmed with what was going on. Trying to cope with all the devastation and all the hopelessness everyone was experiencing had a way of making them resistant to anybody doing anything at any time. The world just wasn't working for them.

John Kees, a member of Berea Christian Church in Russellville, Kentucky, shared a beautiful, philosophical interpretation of why Westside so often seems to work well when "official" efforts by governmental agencies seem to fail:

> *Disaster response from a government at its roots is a failure. It takes grassroots people and individuals to truly accomplish the work. When you are out of your home, you just can't fathom how poor the government's response is. Without being here [in New Orleans] firsthand there is no way to comprehend the devastation and loss that is still here and how, even after five years, things could still be in the condition they're in.*

Dave Lunsford also shared his reflections on the great difficulties that disasters present to governmental agencies that are not flexible enough to respond effectively:

> *I've learned that government entities have excessive procedures and policies that far too often simply get in the way of simply helping people. People who live through disasters do not remember the names of the agencies that support or help them, but they do remember peoples' faces. They may not remember your name, but the faces are what they remember. "You were down here last month to help, weren't you?" "I remember you were here before."*

When people hear about the resistance we encountered from local officials, they ask if that changed over the years, if perhaps Westside and its volunteers eventually became better accepted. I think I should answer "yes" and "no" to that question. In some ways the people of New Orleans as a whole were very appreciative of what we as volunteers did. Often I had folks who have traveled here in church buses tell me that residents stopped them and very sincerely expressed their gratitude to them for coming down.

On the other hand, the tradespeople, the people that you have to work with when you're building homes—the electrical contractors, the plumbing contractors, the heating and air contractors—always remained very insular, overly protective of their working environment. That was really a shame, because that's not something we usually encounter in most other parts of the country. In most places, reciprocity is the order of the day. Reciprocity, the idea of "we'll help you build your business and send work your way and you help enable our volunteer work," was virtually non-existent in New Orleans when we were trying to help with rebuilding. It's a problem that could have crippled our work if we had let it. Sometimes the demands placed upon us as we were forced to deal with contractors drained a lot of our limited resources.

Then there was the challenge of dealing with the people who in the final analysis were the recipients of our mission efforts. With them, there was an ongoing educational process. As a voluntary Christian mission worker and builder, I have to help those I'm ministering to understand that we just don't have a bottomless pit of resources.

With those we seek to help through rebuilding, we

sometimes faced resistance in two respects. First, we encountered a number of people who are part of what some have called the "entitlement generation." Those are folks whose attitude is, "I need it. You have it. You owe it to me and have no right not to give it to me."

Once a group of volunteers came in from working on a couple homes we were rebuilding. They told me about a person who lived next door to one of those sites—a person I had not met—who came out and interrupted them and demanded that they clean up something in front of her house. This had nothing to do with the house they were rebuilding. It was essentially stopping a total stranger and insisting that person help you. The volunteers were very good-hearted about helping. They did what this stranger told them to do. Then the homeowner came back out, criticized what they had done and told them what else she wanted them to do.

I've found it very, very difficult to work with those who have that outlook. At the same time, I have to look at it and say, "Despite that attitude, they still need our help." It's just harder for me to work with them. They seem to believe that their feeling of entitlement in the end is going to get them everything they want. They don't seem to grasp that their attitude itself prevents people from wanting to give them the help they need.

The second group of people we worked with were those who want a "hand-up not a handout." These tend to be the people who, for me, are easier to work with. Still there are real challenges in ministering to them. To begin with, like the entitlement people, the hand-up people have no resources. It's challenging to work with them because they've lost everything they had. And in a very real sense, they're homeless. They may be staying in a dwelling that belongs to somebody else, but until they are back in their houses, they perceive themselves to be homeless.

In working with these displaced homeowners, we found it was often as much a struggle for the mission volunteers as it was for the recipients of their work. Often volunteers come in thinking, "We're going to fix these people's problems and put them back in their homes."

It doesn't take long for volunteers to become immersed in the process and to discover just how much it takes to rebuild a home. Yet even then, the volunteers still say, "Why can't we finish so they can move in?"

At the same time the homeowner is saying, "I want you to get finished today so I can move in tomorrow."

As the mission director, you have to be tremendously understanding as you deal with this tension. You have to walk the line between what we— the volunteers, the homeowner and I—really want to do and what we have the ability, time and funds to do. Over the years, that has been a tremendous challenge for us, one we continue to face every day. You say to yourself, "These are the available, limited resources I have, and here is the overwhelming work I have yet to finish. What do I do? I can't satisfy all of these needs."

Understanding what resources were available—and that their availability was going to change, that it would come and go on a daily basis—was a real learning experience for us as well. We had to learn to be flexible in how the mission center was going to work. We had to learn how to shift our basic approach as our circumstances changed.

In the beginning, we thought basically we would

have people coming down to do mission work. They were giving up their time and bringing resources to help with the rebuild, we assumed. From that perspective, our desire was to give them a place to stay and to give them food to eat while they were here to work. We learned quickly that Week of Compassion (WOC) did not have the depth of resources to allow our original conception to come to real fruition. They were extremely generous in giving us a grant, but they simply did not have the funds to let us provide food and shelter for all our volunteers.

At a certain point, WOC workers came back to us and said, "We can help you with the grant we committed and we can help you with some of your utilities, but we don't have the resources to feed the volunteers who are coming to Westside."

As an aside, I should note that, for all the open-handed giving of Disciples congregations to WOC and for all its efficiency and willingness to move those resources immediately to where they are needed, WOC has limited resources with which to respond to disasters. The catastrophic destruction experienced by New Orleans, Hurricanes Katrina and Rita was so big—and it continues to be huge—that the resources developed through WOC fell way short of what was truly needed to do the job. Because of that, we had to change things around so that the volunteers brought their own food. We thought we could provide the place and all the necessities to do mission work in New Orleans, but we simply could not.

To be candid, we actually ran out of the initial WOC grant money in 2007, but for more than three years, we still managed to keep Westside Mission Center going. The initial money given to us by WOC helped with administration, overhead and operating expenses. There are a lot more expenses involved in a project like this than most people realize. For instance, the cost of insurance here is exorbitantly higher in New Orleans than it is in other places. We had to have flood insurance on the mission property if we wanted to keep operating. We had to have help with that. Those are the kind of things WOC helped us with at the beginning, and we were very grateful for it.

As far as resource money to do our rebuilding jobs, those funds came in large measure from congregations and individuals who made donations. They also came from our collaboration with other organizations that received funding from a variety of sources. I learned early on, and it remained true to a large degree, our greatest success came from working with those displaced homeowners who had received some measure of help from one source or another. Some of those we've helped received assistance either through the Road Home Grants (a federal program that assists certain homeowners), through an insurance payment or from some other source.

Willie Foxworth was a good example of what I'm talking about. As I recall, it cost a little more than $30,000 for the materials to rebuild his house. For the most part Willie paid that. The volunteers from Westside Christian Mission furnished the labor to do his house. So it was a collaborative effort with the homeowner. This is what I mean by the "hand-up not handout." This is how it worked with a large percentage of the people we assisted.

All forms of WOC assistance completely ran out as of April 2009. Beginning at that point in order to keep the mission doors open and the lights on, we started charging a bunk fee. This means the volunteers who came down to Westside paid $75 per person per week as a registration fee. That's the money that kept the mission going day-to-day. It paid our insurance and administrative costs and the upkeep and those sorts of expenses.

Beginning at the same time in 2009, the Great River Region Executive Committee asked me to become a Regional Pastor. Being a Regional Pastor meant I only drew a portion of my salary from Westside. The larger portion of my salary came from the Great River Region. When the region made that move, my job was split 50/50. Fifty percent of my efforts were directed toward mission, and half of that fifty percent—which was roughly a quarter of my time—was focused on Westside Mission Center. Another quarter of my time was directed toward mission work in the region and mission work in the Dominican Republic. The Great River Region has become global mission partners with the Dominican Republic, something I'll discuss more fully in Chapter 6. Of course, fifty percent of my overall time was spent serving as Regional Pastor to forty-seven congregations in mid Mississippi and eastern Arkansas.

It's amazing to remember how mission work was just a dream for me a few years ago and how it became an integrated part of all my ministry. Westside was the heart and the instigation of this, though clearly our vision for the true mission of Westside changed. As it changed, my understanding of what it was going to become—where the Spirit was leading us—also had to be transformed right along with it.

The exterior nearly finished, it's time for a new steeple to grace the Westside sanctuary.

Keith Strain, the pastor of First Christian Church in Crawfordsville, Indiana, has written about coming to Westside as a volunteer when we were in the early stages of rebuilding the facility itself. He wrote about his skepticism and how it was transformed by the awareness of how God was at work in what was happening:

> *I first met Vance Moore Memorial Day weekend of 2006. We had gone with the desire to help with the rebuilding of New Orleans. We were met by a stereotypical Southerner—easy smile, gift for gab, long drawl and backwoods colloquialisms. Vance had a big dream of what could happen to Westside, a congregation with barely any members and a destroyed sanctuary. As he spun out this vision of a rebuilt church and a long-term mission station, I confess that I*

thought he was full of it.

Oh, the vision was noble enough, desirable and needed, but...how?

Well he knew a friend who... And there was a group in Texas that would... And of course, as always, "the Lord will provide."

We spent a week in the unforgiving sun of early summer, building things that were temporary facilities for the groups coming during the summer to tear down the sanctuary and erect the mission center. The only thing that remains of that week of work was the storage shed we built.

That too told me something about Vance. He wanted this shed built on what had been the pad for the air conditioner compressors. I asked Vance what he wanted us to do and he said, "You can figure it out."

Once we got all the old equipment hauled off, we found the slab was not level, dropping from one corner to the opposite corner a good four inches.

Going to Vance again, he gave me the same reply. I thought I was being asked to build the NOLA equivalent of the Leaning Tower of Pisa.

Since then I have learned many things about Vance and the ten trips we have made to Westside.

First of all, he is willing to trust in both the willingness and the capabilities of those who come to aid in the work. Whether he was testing my ability as a builder or not, he knew he could not do everything, and he has had to rely on the volunteers to carry their weight. The effect of this on me and on the groups I have brought is that we assume that we are there to not only do work, but to do good work.

Vance adds another dimension to this, he wants all who come through Westside to understand that they are about good work, that what we are doing is more than helping people in need, we are there as God's hands, God's presence, and God's love.

While that is important, giving to our efforts a sense of calling and divine purpose, Vance adds still another layer of meaning. He insists that volunteers keep their eyes, ears and hearts open to what we can learn from those we come to help.

And as I've constantly said, from the day I first heard about Westside there was a flood of serendipitous God Thangs. One fellow who witnessed and was part of hundreds of those little miracles is Don Miller of Community Christian Church in Manchester, Missouri. It was truly a confluence of unexpected, astonishing events that first brought him to Westside, as he described it:

It was a God Thang that initially brought us to Westside. After Hurricane Katrina, our church had a bunch of people interested in going to help. Making a mission trip was my idea, so I was made the director. It started out to be youth trip. There was an area wide discussion with youth leaders. I was new to mission ministry. I didn't know it worked that way: it's your idea so you're in charge.

In September or October of 2005, we started looking into it seriously and found out there would be no infrastructure for a large mission trip by the summer of 2006. So we turned away from the idea of helping in the hurricane affected areas. Instead, we decided to go to Nebraska for church build. We had forty-three youth lined up for the mission trip in the first week of June 2006. In March, the church build was called off.

We had all these people ready to go on a mission trip and needed someplace to go. We had a phone conversation about this with Carl Zerwick [from the Division of Homeland Ministries]. Carl called back two days later and said, "We can do this, but we'll have to split you up among a whole bunch of different churches with ten to twelve people in any one church and no two churches closer than 50 miles from each other." We didn't want to break our group up that way. Carl said there was one other possibility. There might be a place big enough for us all to go together, but it would take one more week to find out if it would actually materialize. Of course, he was talking about Westside. That was when Vance was in the process of taking over. Only six weeks before we were supposed to leave on the trip, Carl called back with arrangements.

Little did I know what we were walking into. Some of the original group were afraid to go to NOLA, so we ended up with thirty-six people. Carl Zerwick came down as well. We did the initial demolition to the old church building. We were the second group in there. The first group built the shed and emptied out the church. We did the majority of the demolition of the sanctuary. Nobody was allowed inside without a respirator. Half of our group was middle school and high school young people. We ate in a tent—outside in June. We arranged to have our showers outdoors, behind the corner of a building with black plastic shielding.

Beyond the experience of the people, we worked with and those residents we met, the biggest God Thang had to do with the project I was assigned by Bro. Vance. The very first week we were there, we were trying to dismantle the sanctuary so we could save and reuse as much of it as possible. I was a carpenter and contractor. Apparently, it became clear to Vance that I knew what I was doing. I was put in charge of taking the old faceted glass windows out of the sanctuary because we were going to save them.

I looked at Carl Zerwick and Vance and asked, "Are you kidding me?" The wood was termite infested. We were going to try to it save for a year.

Carl Quicksal and I spent four or five days taking those windows out. We cut whole windows out. Finally, we got down to the two big stained glass at the end of the wall above the current baptistery. Those pieces (four of them) were 5' x 6'6" and weigh about 150 pounds. One of the frames was completely eaten apart.

I said, "There is no way we can do this without them breaking."

Somehow, we got them out in one piece. I still don't know how we did that. It took six guys to pick the thing up and move it. Got it set off to the side and then we left.

I was there for my fourth trip in January, 2007. We were working on the sanctuary again. Carl spent the whole week framing and setting the old glass in the sanctuary. That glass had to have been moved at least 20 times after we took it out. Only one of the pieces had any breakage whatever. Still can't believe we did it.

As we were putting in glass, Pat Burke [one of the key leaders of the congregation] came in and broke down. She turned to Carl and said, "My church is back." That project and that moment are so indicative of what happens down there. Things happen down there that defy logic. Things just happen.

Painstakingly protected and moved multiple times, the original stained glass of the old building is installed in the new Westside.

Throughout this book, I talk a lot about folks being transformed through experiences of critical presence that continually occurred at Westside. It's only fair to repeat that I experienced that transformation personally. People saw what God was doing in my life. I think sometimes that helped others, both the volunteers and the people we worked with, be more open to God. I was reminded of this reality when I read what Tom Russell wrote about observing me during the rebuilding of the Westside sanctuary:

> *I've been asked that question so often heard at Westside, "Where did you see God?" One of the first places I saw what God was doing was when we worshipped together in the Westside sanctuary once it was finally dried in. I saw it in the faces and expressions of everyone in the circle and especially in the face of Bro. Vance. I could tell he was seeing one of his visions physically completed.*

Someone asked me if "everybody else kept up?" That is, were the individual donors and the denominational leaders able to keep pace with all the changes Westside went through and were they able to support the changes? I suppose I'd have to say there were those people who got it and those people who didn't.

Surprisingly to a large degree the people who had trouble understanding our emerging mission at Westside were denominational people. Through what was then the Office of Disciple Volunteers—today it's called Disciple Volunteers, the denomination sent workers to the Gulf Coast and set up a group of five mission stations. These stations were initially intended to function only for a period of one year. Some of them were extended, even for as long as four years. Some of them closed as initially planned. These mission stations were created, funded and administered strictly through the Office of Disciples Volunteers.

Westside Mission Center on the other hand was solely a creation of the Great River Region. We believed from the outset our mission was for the long haul. We were working independently of the denominational mission sites. Soon we became a 501(c)3 non-profit corporation, like a congregation. The denominational sites were not established or run like Westside. Because of the differences between us, there was a tremendous lack of understanding between people at the denominational level and people at the Westside Mission level about our charter, our procedures and our expectations.

Michael Elmore has also written about encountering this difficulty:

> *The most frustrating part of all this for me was dealing with some folks in the general church who came with their own agenda and mindset about who we are and what we need. It is still an issue I struggle with and which has a negative impact upon some of our churches.*

In his essay, *What I Learned From Disciple Disaster Response to Katrina, Rita, Gustav and Ike*, Michael wrote:

> *I also learned that actions of some of our well-intended general units could also cause another kind of "second disaster." Some general units came with the mindset that "we are the experts, you all are the victims and we are the ones in charge." There was no discussion of "critical presence"—meaning,*

"what are your needs, how can we work together, how can we help you recover and how can we walk through this with you?"—but the attitude "we are the experts, so just do as we say." This caused a "disaster" of its own that extended for months.

I wonder to this day why there was such misunderstanding. Perhaps it was an educational thing: we did not properly explain to the denominational leaders what we were and what we were attempting to do. Regardless, the Great River Region started Westside Christian Mission as an intentional part of our mission program for service in the region. Westside grew from that point forward and we became a substantial force in the New Orleans community helping the community recover by putting people back into their homes.

Many of the mission stations had members of Disciples churches coming to them and volunteering to take part in the recovery effort, just as Westside did. The difference was that the projects they were working on and the resources they were using predominantly came from outside the denomination, often from organizations like the United Methodist Church and others. Westside was organized and operating differently. The Department of Home Missions (DHM, the general unit that oversees Disciples Volunteers) office, however, tended to treat us as if we were doing the same thing their sites were doing—which ran directly counter to our initial "memorandum of understanding" (MOU).

At times, the manner in which people were being referred to us from the general offices in Indianapolis, with the anticipation that Westside functioned like the other mission sites, created tension. There was a lack of understanding about how Westside Mission Center was proceeding with rebuild efforts we undertook. The denominational leaders, I think, also got frustrated with us because we just didn't do things the way they thought we should.

It should be noted that, despite our shortcomings and frustrations as the people of God, all the volunteers who came to New Orleans in the aftermath of Katrina through our mission centers really made a profound, positive difference. Bob Sieck of Downey Avenue Christian Church in Indianapolis expressed it so well when he said:

> *Disaster response requires a tremendous amount of coordinated effort. I am thankful for the effort the Disciples made to set up the five mission centers in the early days. It is clear to me that without the effort of the faith community, much that has been accomplished in the recovery effort simply would not have happened.*

I was also asked recently if I had been conscious of God's hand at work in the way we established the mission. The clear, short answer to that is "yes." God is *the* presence in my life. We knew—not just me, but Jeannie and I both knew—God's hand was at work in what we were doing. Barb Jones, who has been my mentor now for fifteen years, certainly knew it too.

We knew that we were doing a God Thang. Yes, we had a lot of fun with the saying painted on the wall in the bunkhouse: "It's a God Thang." As I reflect on it, from the very beginning point, we knew God was working through us. When we weren't sure we could even put something together in six months, God moved in people's hearts and we put it together in a week. That was the beginning of knowing this was a God Thang, and all along the way we witnessed God's hand at work every day.

By late in the summer of 2007, the beautiful new sanctuary was nearly complete.

So many times people struggle with the question, "Am I doing God's will?" We didn't have to ask that question as we rebuilt the church and established the mission center. Talk about experiencing God's presence—there were so many times that we needed resources and I would go to bed at night not having any idea where the money was going to come from to do what had to be done the next day. I'd wake up the next morning and somebody would hand me a check or somebody would offer us resources or somebody would call and say, "How can I help?" It was so clear that

God's hand was there. That was the case every miraculous day for the five years at Westside Mission Center.

Chapter 4

Prominently displayed on the walls of the Westside Mission Center in large, vivid letters were a number of slogans and sayings. These phrases were all painted there not because someone thought they were good thoughts and we should adopt them, but because they were those expressions we heard repeated daily—like, "It's a God Thang"—that described our experiences at Westside.

One of the best known phrases painted on the bunkhouse wall was a question that got asked almost every night when groups were doing mission work and staying at Westside. The question was, "Where did you see God today?" It was asked so often that people began to inquire, "Brother Vance, when did you first start asking the volunteers that question?"

It all goes back to when I was lying in the trailer one night, the famous little camper where Jeannie and I spent so many nights. We had torn down the building where the mission center sits today. For some reason, I rolled over and looked out the window. I knew there was nothing out there but this blank slab. We had left a three-inch conduit pipe protruding up through the slab because it connected to another part of the property. That was to be the "pull tube" through which we would access electrical lines and I didn't want to destroy it. When I rolled over that night and gazed out the window, there was a cross tied to that pole. I do not to this day know where it came from, but I saw God in that moment. It was not only the genesis of the famous question but also of what came to be another common practice of mission groups.

Assembling the girders for the bunkhouse, where the mysterious cross appeared.

We had a group in from Saint Louis, Missouri, that week. The following morning I talked with them about the mysterious cross. Although we did not have any of the new building constructed yet, they took some of the material from the building we had just torn down and fashioned it into a cross as they were preparing to leave. They painted it and signed it. And they said, "When the new mission center goes up, this cross will be on the walls." The volunteers who came after them honored that request. They started a tradition that has carried on throughout the life of the mission center.

Sometimes people left crosses. Sometimes they left various things they had decided to build—wooden cutouts of state maps or symbols that had special meaning to the members of the groups; t-shirts created for their group and signed by all the members; decorations created from their construction site tools and materials.

Many folks also wrote on the unpainted beds in the bunkhouse where the volunteers slept. They wrote poems, testimonials and comments. Often people searched for the bunks where they slept in previous years so they could add the dates of their later trips to what they'd written. I never made any suggestions about the things people left. I think it was their unique way of saying, "We were here. We made an impact and this experience has made an impact on us."

I recall a fellow asking me once at one of the ministerial meetings in New Orleans how many members we had at Westside. This was probably at the end of the first year and Westside had ten or fifteen members. When he asked me, "Vance, how many members you got," I heard myself saying, "Well, about 1500."

He said, "Give me a break, man. I've seen your church. You couldn't get 1500 people in there if you stacked them up."

And I said, "Sure I can."

He said, "How do you do it?"

"About thirty or forty of them at a time," I said. "And if you do that every week, pretty soon you got 1500 of them." I really believe that. And there came a point where we had more than 4000.

People came to the Westside Mission Center and they had the transforming experience I've talked so much about—and which, by the way, is the same thing that can happen in your local church. We brought people into an environment of worship and service. We shared the love of Christ with them. We had an experience with them that changed them at the deepest level, and we became family. We became God's family.

That's what this thing is all about. It always has

been. In fact, if you're willing to do it, you can go back and look at the origins of the Campbell-Stone moment from which our denomination, the Christian Church (Disciples), came and you'll see that's the way it all began.

When you take away this obsession we church folks have with numerical membership and you strive to impact people for Christ instead of impacting people for "First Christian Church of Anywhere, USA," you begin to build the Kingdom of God. That in all candor is exactly what we did at Westside.

This dynamic spirituality was not only obvious among volunteers and members of Westside Christian Church, but we also saw similar, incredible transformations among the people we were assisting. This is not to say that all these people—homeowners and volunteers alike—were not worthy and admirable before their association with the mission center. It has been as if God took the good foundations of their lives and built upon them. In each case, those who experienced these transformations found the way they live and the way they perceive the world to be dramatically changed.

While I'm discussing dramatic changes, I should take a moment and talk about the spring and summer of 2007 and the transformation that touched my life in a special way. Of course, I'm speaking about the loss of my wife Jeannie.

For sixteen months, she lived out the answer to the prayer she prayed before that last major surgery in Arkansas. During that time, her spirit and her work became a tremendous example of Christian faith to thousands of volunteers and to the members of Westside Christian Church who came to love her so much. For as long as she could, to the extent she could,

Jeannie was completely active in our work. For as long as the mission center was open, the wall hanging she made for the bunkhouse still hung there with the initials "JOY": "Jesus, Others, You." Jeannie lived by that slogan.

Adorning the wall of the bunkhouse, along with the remembrances of many volunteer groups, the JOY banner created by Jeannie remained as long as the center was open.

We were not in New Orleans long before we became aware that her cancer had returned. On April 25, 2007, the doctor told us to call in hospice. Jeannie and I knew she would not live long after that. Of course, we had known when we moved to New Orleans that she would die there.

The congregation experienced her death with a combination of undeniable sadness and a real sense of salvation. On the south side of the sanctuary, they constructed a small flower garden, dedicated it to

Jeannie and placed a lovely marker there in her memory. Eventually they took the step of dedicating the bunkhouse to Jeannie and me.

Her memorial service was truly a celebration of her life. Many new friends were present, those had she made among the congregation and even volunteers who made another trip down to Westside to remember her and rejoice in her life.

Tom Sikes wrote a letter about that period of time and described what was happening in such a beautiful way:

> *The parsonage was completed just a few weeks before Jeannie died. Vance gathered us all at her bedside and we had a brief worship service of thanksgiving for Jeannie. Children, adults and this couple huddled in hope and it was indeed a holy pause. David in his psalms called it "Selah." And that's what it was for those of us involved. This Selah moment continues to remind me of God's critical presence on the road between suffering and hope. Vance serves in it. Vance and Jeannie lived in it.*

Don Miller also recalled that time:

> *I've been to New Orleans seventeen times, but only once by myself. That was when I went for Jeannie's funeral. I was honored to be asked to speak. Before the funeral, I did some work. I helped lay sod before the service so the church would look really good.*

Jeannie died on July 3, 2007. Ten days later, on

Friday, July 13, a memorial service was held in her honor at Westside Christian Church. How grateful I was and still am for our family, many colleagues and brothers and sisters in Christ who were present for the celebration of her life.

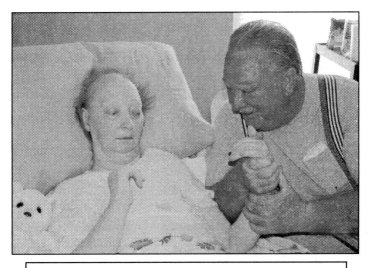

In her last moments, Jeannie affirmed she was going to be with Jesus -- and asked Vance if he wanted to come along.

During the last days of her life and the days that followed, the work of Westside continued unabated. This was important and it was difficult. I wanted to take some time off from the work we were doing to be alone with my thoughts and to fulfill promises I had made to Jeannie. Circumstances forced me to remain close to the mission site. As I reflect upon it now, I recognize the Spirit of God sustained me during those difficult weeks. To be sure, Jeannie would have wanted me to take care of myself, but also to make sure Westside Mission Center continued its work. Indeed the work of Westside was moving into a new direction:

returning displaced owners to their homes.

One of the first homeowners we assisted, Dee Jones, is a fine example of what I'm describing. At the time I first met her, we were working on the Westside church facility as well as gutting some other properties. We were not doing complete rebuilds at the time—just a little of this and a little of that. One day I was approached by Chandra Jones, who was with a volunteer group from a church in Frankfort, Kentucky. Chandra had taken some of the people in her group up and down Delery Street in the Lower Ninth Ward. While they were there, they met Dee's ex-husband, Alan, who apparently told Chandra enough of Dee's story to create quite an impact. Chandra came back to me and said, "You have got to go and talk to this woman over on Delery Street."

I did not particularly want to go. After all, we already had more work than we could do. So I told the people from Frankfort I would go talk to her, but that I would not help her. I explained we were too far behind with the jobs we'd already committed to do and I certainly didn't have the time to take on any new projects.

When I went over to talk to her and drove up to her address on Delery Street, I saw a house that had been gutted. Only the roof, the exterior brick walls and the interior studs remained over the concrete foundation. Out front, there was a great mound of trash that had been the insides of her house: her furnishings and her personal possessions. I saw a FEMA trailer that had not been wired for electricity. And in front of this desolation, I saw a woman who was working in her flowerbed.

Imagine if you will an empty, derelict house that bad been inundated twice by floodwater, with a mountain of trash for a front yard, in the middle of a neighborhood that looked as bad as any third world country you have ever seen in pictures. Up in the planter in the front of the house, however, flowers were growing. I don't know how many different plants there were. I remember the red ones because I thought they were pretty.

I was looking at those flowers as I walked up and introduced myself to her. I told her who I was and that I had promised I would speak to her. My mindset was to be polite, to look at her house and to tell her the truth: "Ain't no way I can get around to helping you, even if we did this kind of rebuilding work."

We exchanged pleasantries. She shared with me that she couldn't live in the FEMA trailer because they hadn't inspected it. So there was no power. She was staying over with her ex-husband while she was waiting to get the electricity turned on.

Westside volunteers installing woodwork in the home of Dee Jones. Note the FEMA trailer on the left.

Above all, she was trying everything within her power to get her house rebuilt. She had only received $10,000 in compensation and she had been taken advantage of by a contractor whose sole contribution to her house was a set of ill-fitting windows.

Her story, to be sure, was very typical. By that time, I had already heard many tales like hers. As I discussed in Chapter 2, there was a tremendous amount of contractor fraud in the aftermath of Katrina. People weren't getting very much money and unscrupulous individuals were cheating them out of it. What Dee related to me was just another page in the plethora of heartache and problems New Orleans residents were facing. I was standing there listening to her, thinking that her story was basically not much different than anybody else's. Only I couldn't stop thinking about those flowers.

As we stood in front of the house talking, I finally said, "I have got to ask you about the flowers. They are a bright spot in the midst of total desolation and I don't understand. What's the deal?"

She said to me, "I had $5 left in my pocket. I was down at Home Depot, dreaming about fixing my house. They had these flowers and I could buy them for $5. I made up my mind I was going to come up here and I was going to work in my flowerbed. This is my home and I'm coming back to it. These flowers tell that story. I'm coming back. Nothing is going to stop me from coming back to my house."

I guess you could say those flowers were a God Thang. As I looked at that woman, I saw a level of determination that inspired me and touched my heart. I had just heard her tell me about getting almost no help—and what little assistance she received had been taken from her. Yet here she was, so full of faith that she was working in the flowerbeds.

I guess Dee was like the prophet Ezekiel, exiled in Babylon but still buying property in the Holy Land. Although he had absolutely no logical reason to believe the circumstance of his people would ever change, he still had faith that he and his ancestors would one day return to the homes God had given them. Dee was just like Ezekiel, making a stand to say, "I am not going to be defeated."

It came to me right then that, if she had that much faith—and that's all she had was faith—then God must've sent me there to give her a ray of hope. So I did. It was pretty clear what I needed to do. I made the commitment right then we would help her rebuild her house.

That was also a God Thang, I suppose, in the sense that it marked the beginning of Westside rebuilding homes rather than just tearing them down. It was another step we took. The Spirit was transforming our mission as we went about answering God's call to serve.

To fully appreciate the situation you have to realize that, at the time I committed us to work on Dee's house, we didn't have any money. I went back to the mission center that night. The group from Kentucky was there—the very group that sent me over to see her.

I said to them, "I need some help. I don't have any money and I want to help Dee Jones."

After I explained the circumstances to these folks, they put together—if my memory serves me correctly—somewhere around $400 to $500. I don't know where that money came from. It certainly wasn't something they intended to give. They just pulled it together. It was a God Thang. Then we went over to Dee's house and just started working, which I think is what you're supposed to do when you experience a God Thang.

Each morning, volunteers crossed the Mississippi River on the ferry to travel to job sites.

Something else started at that point I had never anticipated. As other groups came in following the folks from Frankfort, they would either bring money and ask where it could be used, or I would describe to them what we were doing at Dee's house and the next thing you know, they would have a contribution to make. Beginning that first night, whenever I asked for help, the resources were always there. I know the Spirit made it so. It's a God Thang.

There's something else I think I should inject here. When I answered the call to ministry, I remember as if it were yesterday saying to God in prayer: "I'll do anything you ask me to do, Father. I will go anywhere you ask me to go. There is only one thing I will not do. I will never, ever, ever ask anybody for money."

How strange I feel admitting that. The only "never" left in my vocabulary is I hope I *never* take a stand and tell God what I won't do.

At that point in the work coming from Westside Mission Center, transformations were already taking place. Miraculous God Thangs were abounding. I thought often of the Book of Acts in the New Testament and how the Spirit's transforming power through the work of the apostles repeatedly proved to be contagious. I also discovered that the transforming power of the Spirit was contagious among residents of New Orleans through the work of our Westside volunteers.

We're working on the house one day and this very quiet older gentleman came and introduced himself to me. He told me his name was Willie Foxworth. He had come over to cut the grass for Dee. He did it out of the goodness of his heart because she didn't have a lawnmower. She also didn't have any money and the grass was really growing. She was a single lady who needed some help and he just came and helped her.

Willie watched us as we worked on Dee's house. He had a house over on another street. When he saw the quality of work we did, he decided he wanted us to come fix his house as well.

I said, "Sir, I don't have time to come fix your house. I'm busy."

He said, "That's all right, I'll wait."

I said, "You may have to wait six months."

He said, "I'll wait. I want you to fix my house."

Willie explained he had been watching the volunteers. Not only was he impressed with their work, but somehow he just knew we were the ones who were supposed to fix his house. So Willie waited until the time came we could work on his house.

As we got toward end of our work on Dee's house and we were about to get her moved in, I realized it was time to come to an understanding with our next homeowner. So I sat down and talked to Willie. By that time, I had already checked him out and I knew he was someone we were going to be able to help. He had received some Road Home grant money. I knew he didn't get enough to rebuild his house if he had been forced to use a regular contractor. Though I knew about how much money he had received, he didn't know that I knew.

So I went to him and I said, "Willie, here's the way we do it. You furnish the material and I'll furnish the labor and I'll rebuild your house. I'll do it right. I won't do it fancy. I will do it right because that's the way we do it."

He came right back at me. "Now here's the way I want to do it. You want me to pay for the materials. Okay, we'll go down to Home Depot and I'll buy 'em."

I said, "No, I ain't got time for that. I'll buy the materials and I'll bring you the tickets and you pay me back."

Then he said, "That's a fair deal."

I learned a lesson from that I really feel the need to share. I learned the depth of the pride possessed by these human beings we found ourselves helping. By in large, I don't think people outside this situation truly grasp the integrity and sincerity of these people we are assisting. Understanding their fortitude and pride in the face of what they've endured is something that can't help but change your perspective.

After our agreement, the volunteers got started on Willie's house. It was a complete rebuild because it had been completely destroyed. We started from the slab and worked our way up until we finished.

The first Friday morning, Willie called me and said, "I want to pay my bill."

I said, "We'll get together Monday."

He said, "No. You said we'd settle up on Friday. I want to pay my bill."

So I added up the tickets. I gave him a copy of them and put a copy in my file. Willie paid me—in cash.

I said, "Willie, I don't like cash. It's hard for me to deal with, especially since you insist on paying every Friday."

So he went down and he started a checking account. That's how we proceeded each week: I'd bring him the tickets; I would fill out the amount; he would sign the check. That went on until we finished the job.

Now I knew Willie got $40,000 in Road Homes funds—give or take a penny one way or the other. As we consider that, I think it's important to recognize that, when these homeowners got money, it had to cover everything they lost. With a storm like Katrina, a guy like Willie lost his pots and pans and his BVD's all at the same time. Most of the residents of New Orleans got out with nothing more than the clothes on their back. So I tried very, very hard to rebuild Willie's house with as much stewardship in mind as I could. The better I conserved money, the more money the homeowner had left at the end of the project. That was our attitude with every job we undertook. In Willie's case, we spent about $31,000. I knew that left Willie, give or take, with about $9000.

Then came the last week of the rebuild, the week we had his house ready to be occupied. He didn't have any furniture in it yet, but the house at least was ready to go. I think I had a couple hundred dollars in receipts that he had not yet reimbursed.

Willie called me and said, "I want to settle my bill."

I said, "Willie, I've got another house going and I'm real, real busy. I'd appreciate it if you just wouldn't worry about it right now. It's only a couple hundred dollars. We'll get together later."

He said, "Well, okay."

A couple times during the next week I heard from Willie. He wanted to pay his bill. I put him off because I was extremely busy.

Then came an evening after I had been out on the job with some volunteers and we had really been working hard. It was summertime. It was hot and I was sweaty. I was tired. I dragged myself into the parsonage and said "Hi" to my two old dogs, then I just sat down on the couch. I was whipped. I picked up my guitar. All I wanted to do was rest. As the man says, "I'm 'laxing."

All of a sudden there came a knock on the door. I could see through the little oval window in the door it was Willie. I went over and opened it up and I said, "Hey, Willie."

He said, "I come to pay my bill."

I said, "Willie, I'll get the money later. I'm tired."

He said, "No. Come out here."

His old van was parked out in the street in front of the parsonage and I walked out there with him. Willie opened the door and reached on up on the dashboard. The check was already made out this time. He handed it to me and I saw it was for $7000.

I said, "Willie, what is this?"

He said, "You 'hoped' me. I want you to 'hope' somebody else."

I said, "Willie, I know much money you got left. You ain't got but $9000 and you got to buy furniture and all kinds of other stuff."

He just looked at me and said, "Don't you worry about what I got to buy. God told me to give you $7000 and that's what I'm doing."

I said, "Willie, I'm not going to take your money."

He just looked at me, crawled up in the cab of that truck and he said, "Don't argue with me. Argue with God. He's the one told me to do it." And he drove off.

So Westside Mission Center received $7000 from Willie Foxworth. Ultimately, we used it as seed money for the rebuilding of the Greater New Jerusalem Missionary Baptist Church, which I talk about in the next chapter.

As if that were not enough, for as long as the center was open Willie continued to bless Westside with his generosity. This harkens back to how he first found out about us.

Going back to when we first started working on his place in late 2007 or early 2008, Willie came over as often as needed and cutting the grass at the mission center. He does not live near the church, but that did not stop him from coming over regularly. In order to do it, he really had to go out of his way. And from the beginning he refused to accept payment—even money for gas.

Finally, I said, "Willie, you can't keep doing this. You have to let me pay you."

"All right," he said. "You can pay me for gas. I'll give you the bill for the gas I buy."

Somehow, Willie was never as prompt and dependable in giving me his gasoline bills as he expected us to be in submitting receipts for his building supplies.

Now in the 12th Chapter of his letter to the Romans, the Apostle Paul has a series of exhortations. He writes: "Outdo one another in showing honor. Do not

lag in zeal. Be ardent in spirit. Serve the Lord."
[NRSV]

That was the scripture that came to my mind some months after we got that check from Willie, because I had a very similar experience with his brother. It seemed the two were trying to outdo one another in showing their appreciation for Westside and its volunteers.

We weren't able to start work on Willie's house until six months after he first asked. This was because we were in the process of fixing Dee's house, not to mention working on other jobs we had committed to finish. When we finally were able to start on his house, we got to know him a lot better. As we became better acquainted, we found out that he had a brother, an older brother. Soon it came to light that his brother's house had also been destroyed by Katrina and needed to be rebuilt. Then we met Willie's brother Ray and Ray's wife Clara.

In the natural progression of things, we also began to rebuild the home of Ray and Clara Foxworth. As we were doing Ray's house and getting toward the end, he came to me and said, "I want to give you some money."

I said, "Ray, you don't need to give me no money."

Ray said, "Yeah I do. Willie gave you money. I'm going to give you money. How much money did Willie give you?"

I said, "What's that got to do with it?"

He said, "'Cause whatever money Willie give you, I'm going to give you a little more."

I said, "You ain't going to do it. I'm not going to tell you how much money Willie give me."

We went back and forth. Finally Ray ended up giving me, I think, $5600 with instructions to go help somebody else. We put that money to work right away with another rebuild.

Ray and Clara's house was a total loss. When we first started working on it, it had not even been gutted. One of the first groups of volunteers to work on it was a bunch of young men from Wabash College in Indiana. They had given up their spring break, time they could've been at some beach in Florida or Texas, in order to help rebuild homes in New Orleans. Instead of just going down to the coast and enjoying themselves, they worked very hard helping put people's lives back together. I saw God in what they were doing.

One morning we took them over to Ray's house and told them to tear out everything on the inside down to the studs and pile all the refuse in the front yard. We also told them to tear down Ray's old shed behind the house.

"You mean that big shed?" one of them asked, pointing at the crooked structure at the back of Ray's driveway.

"Well that's got to go too," I said. "But that's not Ray's shed. That's a garage from another house that floated onto his property. Ray's shed is under that garage."

Dave Lunsford shared with me a God Thang that emerged from the work the Wabash students did on Ray and Clara's house:

We finished gutting the house and removing the car porch and garden shed that had been destroyed in the hurricane. A small set of garden tools was found and we brought them back home with us. We had them cleaned up and the following year we gave them back. Even though it was just a small set of tools that had already been replaced, we could see the tears in Ray's eyes. One small piece of his former life was restored. His gratitude was overwhelming, over a few tools.

Ray Foxworth's driveway before reconstruction began. Note the neighbor's garage atop the back of the house.

Those were the sort of issues volunteers ran into when they came down to help us with the rebuilding. Just before the Wabash boys began working on the house, a group from Winston-Salem, North Carolina had also been gutting it and found a number of personal effects from Ray and Clara. They heeded the admonition we gave to volunteer groups not to take home Katrina "souvenirs." Instead, they collected the items, things the Foxworth's had long since considered lost to the flood, and gave them to me to return to the owners. Well, they returned all the personal items except one.

As they tore out the kitchen cabinets, Becky

Minnix, one of the North Carolina workers, lifted a random piece of plywood off the counter. Beneath it, sitting in water, was large charcoal portrait of a man. The volunteers discussed what to do. They realized that, without proper care and restoration, this flimsy, soaked paper would just disintegrate. Carefully they sealed the portrait in airtight plastic. Another member of the group, Martha Hutson, took the portrait to Bruce Wilson, an art restorer she knew in Salisbury, North Carolina. She explained what had happened to the charcoal and the significance of it. The expert took on the charcoal as a benevolent work, carefully restoring the portrait and framing it. The restoration and frame had a retail value of $800.

The artwork was discovered in the spring of 2008. The restoration was completed one day before the group left for their third Westside mission trip in 2009. On the day before they were to finish their work and return to North Carolina, the group encountered Willie Foxworth as he was unloading his mower to cut the grass at the mission center. They knew him because they had worked on painting and landscaping at his house the previous year.

"Willie," they asked, "can you tell us who this is a portrait of?"

Very surprised, he replied, "Well, that's my father."

The next day the group took the charcoal over to Ray's house. Of course, Ray still had no idea that they had found the drawing. The group was invited in by Clara and made their presentation. Janice Taylor, an artist who was one of the North Carolina folks, brought the tools and helped Ray and Clara hang the frame in their living room.

This would have been a God Thang in and of itself, but it was made all the more significant when Clara told them that just the day before Ray had been diagnosed with Lou Gehrig's disease. The entire volunteer group was moved and subdued as they got back onto the church bus for their trip home.

Willie Foxworth, right, never ceased being grateful for Westside Mission Center.

Perhaps it is such transforming experiences that drew groups like the Winston-Salem volunteers and the young men from Wabash College back year after year. With such groups—and there were many of them— more and different people came to Westside. The experiences they had, while unique, all resonated with that same powerful awareness of God's transforming power.

In the spring of 2008, some of the Wabash College boys assisted in the construction of a fortress fence around Westside's backyard. As they were digging holes and setting posts in cement, an elderly couple approached them to ask for assistance. This husband

and wife were tourists from Kansas who had come to check out New Orleans on behalf of their church and take back a report of the city's condition. Just prior to leaving Kansas, the woman had a pacemaker implanted to regulate her heart. She was supposed to send daily updates back to her doctor by way of telephone calls. On this particular day, the couple had driven for miles looking around for a place with a landline because a cell phone wouldn't work. For whatever reason, they simply could not find a place with a phone they could use.

As they drove along, becoming more and more anxious, they spotted the Westside Christian Church sign with its red chalice and white cross emblem, the denominational symbol. Being members of the Christian Church (Disciples), they decided to pull onto the parking lot. There they saw the young men of Wabash constructing a fence. The students let them into the educational building where they could access a landline and allow the woman's pacemaker to make its daily update on the condition of her heart. Ironically, it had been several weeks since a group did any work at the church. It was just a coincidence—a God Thang— that the Wabash boys were there that day building the fence.

Over the years, there were more and more occasions when residents of New Orleans showed unreserved gratitude for our volunteers. Many local folks gained a sense of the sacrifices our volunteers made and the things they accomplished. Karen Zuver, a member Hiram Christian Church in Hiram, Ohio, described this dynamic very well:

> *When you come to NOLA from "up north,"*
> *everyone knows it. All you have to do is open*

your mouth. They're glad you're here, as a tourist maybe, when you say, "Well I have been to Bourbon Street and I've eaten beignets. But when you say, "I'm here with the Westside Mission doing reconstruction work with Brother Vance, you know, over in the Lower 9th," that's all it takes for their faces to light up and they are ready to talk to you, even if your accent is from "up north."

Crystin Faenza of Berea Christian Church in Russellville, Kentucky, wrote:

I see God in the smiles on the faces of the people that we encounter every day. From the volunteers to the people being helped, to their neighbors and even to people who pass us on the street and see the work we're doing."

All of these experiences drew me toward a fuller understanding of what I now call critical presence: the intersection of human beings reaching out to help other human beings at the moment of deepest need. This to me is a direct reflection of what Jesus did in the gospels and what the Lord intends for us to do as Christians.

Everything I read in the Bible tells me Jesus ministered to people at moment of critical presence. He went out into the community. As opposed to being with the religious leaders and those in positions of authority, he worked with the disadvantaged. We read stories of Jesus being with outcasts of every sort and helping them; stories of Jesus ministering to the blind, deaf, lame and others who were considered to be physically unacceptable; stories of Jesus working with those judged ethnically, spiritually and physically to be lesser members of society. I think the lesson for us, if we want to be like Jesus—and obviously that's what we're supposed to do—is find people who are in need and fill that need. In the process of doing that, the message of Jesus, the message of love, is carried with us.

As our work at Westside Mission Center progressed and grew more refined, I could see the hand of God at work as volunteers reached out to the handful of homeowners and other individuals we've described in this chapter. The way we did mission at Westside, however, was still growing and developing. I also discovered I was not finished learning about critical presence, about how ministering at that moment can change not just individuals but entire congregations and communities. This is the subject of the next chapter.

Chapter 5

During the time we were working on the home of Dee Jones, we encountered another woman who lived on the corner a few houses down from her. This lady's name was Thelma Tyler. Like everyone else, her house had been inundated by Hurricane Katrina.

Thelma is an elderly widow and she has a real strong personality. For a long time she just sat there on her property watching as different groups of volunteers came and went and Dee's house got rebuilt. Somewhere along the way she decided that we were honest and doing good things. She also decided, before she and I ever spoke, that we were going to do for her what we were doing for Dee. People have asked me about why we agreed to work with Thelma and what it was like. I remind them of the story in the 18th chapter of Luke about the widow and the judge. The widow aggravated the judge until he said, "The only way I'm going to get rid of this woman is to give her what she wants." Well, Thelma was the widow and I was the judge.

I will tell everybody who is interested that I love Thelma dearly. Still, she proved difficult to assist. When we were working on her house, she would call me every morning and give me a list of what she thought needed to be done that day.

I would say, "Thelma, you need to let me do this."

She'd come right back at me. "Well you just need to remember this and remember this."

Apart from dealing with Thelma, working on her house was certainly not easy. If anything could go wrong on a job, it went wrong at Thelma's. The wood was full of termites. We ended up rebuilding that house from the inside out.

Finally one day I was frustrated and aggravated and tired and just being a regular old human being. And Thelma was being Thelma. I decided I just needed to get out of there for a little while. I needed to go find a pastor to talk to for myself.

For some time I had wanted to find a pastor, a colleague, to talk to in the Lower Ninth Ward. All the churches I had seen at that time, because the churches unlike the homeowners didn't get any rebuild money, were sitting there empty. Most of them hadn't even been gutted.

On that particular day, I used it an excuse to get into this big old yellow truck, Big Bird, and just start riding up and down the streets of the Lower Ninth Ward. I came down Bartholomew Street right up to Johnson Street. At that location, I had seen a little old church several times. It kind of stuck in my mind because they had burglar bar doors on it. And I had always thought, "How strange that we have to have iron bars on the doors of a church."

I pulled down the Johnson Street side, the long side of the church. I saw an old SUV sitting out front and I parked the truck. Peeking out at me through the double set of iron bar doors on the front of that church house I saw a little old man. That was the first time I ever saw Pastor Howard Washington of the Greater New Jerusalem Missionary Baptist Church. I had no idea then that one day we would be close friends and he would be an inspiration for me.

I leaned out the truck window and I said, "You the pastor?"

He said, "Yeah."

I said, "Can I talk to you?"

"Yeah." He wasn't being real talkative.
I got out. He was still behind those gates.
I said, "Well can we go inside?"
He said, "Yeah."
He went back inside and I followed him. He sat up on the side of a couple sawhorses.

If you can envision, he had piled up a bunch of old pews he had taken loose from the floor of the sanctuary. You could tell from looking at the bottoms of them that they were coming apart. There were some old two-by-fours that looked as if they had been lying outside somewhere because they had turned gray. There was a gasoline generator, so I knew he didn't have any electrical power in the church. There were the two sawhorses he was sitting on and a Skill saw.

As I looked at the walls about fourteen feet up, I could see the mud and straw that showed how high the floodwater had risen in his sanctuary. He just sat there watching me as I looked around.

I knew that he had been working and trying to fix the place up by himself. I asked, "Pastor, where's your help?"

He just pointed up.

I said, "Well I know, but I'm talking about where are his hands. Where are your helpers?"

He said, "Ah, they ain't showed up yet."

I was already starting to choke up a little bit. This old man and the situation he was facing were beginning to get to me.

"I know, Pastor. I understand," I said. "Can we help you?"

He said, "I ain't got no money."

I should've realized then he thought I was a contractor. But I said, "I realize you ain't got any money, but can we help you rebuild your church?"

And he said, "I *told* you, I ain't got any money."

I was thinking to myself that he had just seen the cross on the side of my truck and the slogan that says, "Brothers and Sisters in Christ Serving." The acronym of that, of course, is BASICS.

So I said to him again, "Pastor, what if I had some material and I had some helpers, could we help you rebuild your church?"

It was almost like I saw a light bulb go off in that old man's eyes. He said, "You *know* that you can help me."

With his back to "Big Bird," the pastor observes the installation of an awning over the front door of the church.

That was a major God Thang. Later I came to understand what had happened. There were times, you see, when we would have to make decisions about how we were going to rebuild the church. I would say, "Pastor what do you want to do about so-and-so?"

He would reply, "Well you just do whatever you

want."

And I would insist, "Pastor, this is your church. This is not my church."

Then he would come back with, "You don't understand. God sent you here to bring this church back. You decide what we do. I don't decide what we do."

He believes that to this day, that God sent me to him to rebuild his church. It came to him like a revelation when I asked if I could bring in materials and volunteers and help him.

There had been a moment after Katrina, after the destruction of his church facility, when one of his sons had said to him, "Daddy, you're an old man. You need to walk out of this building and go home and set on the front porch."

Pastor told him, "As long as I have the breath of life, I will try to bring this church back." I came to realize that Pastor Washington saw us Westside Mission Center workers as the beginning of the fulfillment of that prophecy.

After that first meeting with him, I went back right away and I got volunteers and I came over and we got started. That was on April 2. The reason I remember the date clearly is because I had asked him in that first conversation how old he was. He told me he was seventy-nine-years-old on March 31and this was three days later.

Together Pastor Washington and I set the date of August 11, four months after we began, for the rededication of Greater Jerusalem Church. During those four months, I had probably 1000 people to volunteer. That was during the prime time of the year, the tail end of spring break and soon we would have all the people who were going to spend their summer vacations with us. Sometimes we would have sixty or seventy people in the mission center at a time. We raised $37,000 to redo that church, counting the money that Willie had given and with gifts from the volunteers during that four months.

Volunteers were a little overwhelmed at the scope of damage they found inside Pastor Washington's church.

There are many memories, stories and lessons that spin off the rebuilding of Greater Jerusalem Church, but as I relate this, one thing comes back to my mind in a particular way. I remember this because I had made a commitment to do houses, and this was not a house. It was a house of God, but it was not somebody's home. I knew in my heart that we *had* to rebuild Greater Jerusalem Church. Still I questioned myself often about how many other people we could have helped with the $37,000 of materials we used. Somehow, the Spirit always refocused me on the church. On August the 11, just as we had agreed, we had the rededication of the church. We worked and we finished. And along the way, people's lives were touched and changed.

Something else was built through our effort—a lasting friendship. Howard and I became very close. And as I watched, I saw Howard impact the lives of hundreds if not thousands of volunteers over time.

Jennifer Higgins, a member of the Berea Christian Church of Russellville, Kentucky, wrote me about the God Thang that brought her and her husband Chris to Westside and ultimately made them part of the Greater New Jerusalem rebuilding work:

We were scheduled to take a cruise and it was cancelled, so we were stuck in New Orleans in February, 2007. Because we had lots of extra time on our hands, we opted to take the "Post Katrina Devastation Tour." The despair and devastation we saw moved us deeply. Then we returned home and a number of other things seemed to work together to open our eyes to the need in New Orleans.

In July 2008, a group from our church stepped out of our comfort zone and took our first mission trip ever. We were so incredibly blessed by our experience here working with Brother Vance and Pastor Washington. As I write, we are headed to New Orleans for our third summer and we continue to be blessed every moment we are here.

Berea Christian Church found another remarkable way to assist Greater Jerusalem Church, the sister congregation it never knew it had. In 2008 as the empty sanctuary was nearing completion, members of

Berea remembered the pews they had stored away after the renovation of their own church seven years before. These spare pews actually had great sentimental value to the Berea Christians because they had been in use in Russellville for 100 years before they had been carefully stored away. They contacted a trucker named Sam, also a member of Berea Christian Church, who drove for a factory and regularly delivered carpet supplies from Kentucky to the New Orleans area. His company allowed him to leave enough space on the back of his truck to pack the pews and some additional chairs and deliver them to Greater Jerusalem Church. As we reflected on this development with quiet gratitude, we agreed with one another that this was definitely a God Thang.

I was very interested to read the perspective of Tom Sikes, Pastor of First Christian Church in Meridian, Mississippi, and someone who was already a veteran mission worker by the time he and his volunteers began to help with Greater Jerusalem Church:

> *Vance invited us to go to the Lower Ninth Ward. And so we did. We trusted him and I'm so glad we did. We heard rumors of crime and we were told how crazy we were to go there, but we went by the calling of God and there is no doubt about that.*
>
> *I remember the first time I went there and was met by the pastor, Howard Washington. He led us in a prayer that had the cadence of a well-seasoned man of God.*
>
> *"Father of Abraham, Isaac and Jacob, you have led us through the dark of night to live another day . . . ." We felt as if we were eavesdropping on a holy conversation between*

this man and his God.

We all went to our stations and began working. John Bounds and I went next door to begin cleaning out an apartment that was loaded with materials and junk so the church could eventually use it as an apartment. And it was there in that dark, dank place that I saw Jesus. Jesus was in the form of Pastor Washington, sitting on a five-gallon bucket removing the old plumbing from a bathroom. After Katrina, looters came and stole all the copper from the building, so it had to be replumbed.

Here was a man who had started that church forty years ago and who was still silently and faithfully serving. He was not mad. He was not bitter. He was waiting.

As I thought about the story of how Brother Vance met Pastor Washington at that moment, I remembered Acts 8:26-40, the story of Philip and the Ethiopian. To me, the meeting of those two biblical figures, one dark skinned and one white, both spiritual seekers in a wilderness place yearning to find God's will, was no less miraculous than the meeting of these two modern day men of God. And just as with that ancient story, the results are far reaching.

I sat in that dark bathroom and listened as Pastor Washington, this modern day Jesus, told me his story: "I ran from God for years. My parents told me I was called by God. But I didn't want to follow God. I wanted to do my own thing."

His voice was slow, aged like fine wine. I hung on each syllable. He took out a handkerchief to wipe the sweat from his face in the extreme heat and then he continued. "One night I went to the liquor store to buy me some medicine to ease my pain. I drank it. Then I went to a bar. I came out and ran my car right into the Mississippi River. It was then and there I knew I had to quit my running from God. I gave my life to the call to be a preacher. And here I am now, thankful to God for not giving up on me."

Well, you can imagine the emotion in that room as he spoke. He was reliving his call. I was honored to be hearing his story.

I found out that Pastor Washington built the church forty years ago. His cousin came and painted the baptismal pool wall with the image of two cousins, John the Baptizer and Jesus. It was a striking reminder of the cousins then and now. Of all the things that got destroyed in that storm called Katrina, the church baptismal wall remained intact. How in the world did that happen? The sheetrock was bending in places, but you could still see the figures. It survived the storm. Just like Noah enduring the flood, just like Israel going through the rising waters, pursued by Pharaoh, so with this church and Katrina, the storm of the ages.

The baptistery painting of the baptism of Christ was disintegrating in disrepair.

The back wall of the baptistery Tom was describing had an emotional impact on other volunteers as well. Eleanor Hinson, a high school principal who came with Tom's group, wanted to do something special to preserve that image. While others in her group went to other sites to work, Eleanor asked if she could stay behind and repaint the images on the wall. Her intricate, delicate work brought the "cousins" back to life. As she worked on it, others repaired the sheetrock and the glass front of the baptistery.

Time and again, I saw volunteers "adopt" a particular aspect of a job—like the three medical doctors who invested an entire day to rebuild the door of the Westside supply shed. Volunteers realize they won't be able to complete the entire rebuilding of someone's home, so they focus on finishing the one part of it they can with great love and care.

Workers led by Eleanor Hinson of Meridian, Mississippi, carefully restored the baptistery mural.

For some reason working on the intricate tile floor in the entry of the Greater Jerusalem Church had a profound impact on the folks who invested so much time there. Tom wrote about several people who had God experiences either there or that began there:

Jane Swanson is a woman from our church, a retired teacher, who helped a team of our members working on the tile floor. One tile at a time, Jane guided the team all the way through to completion. With sore necks and hands, she showed us the reality of "critical presence" on her knees. Those who worked alongside her, including a number of our youth, became fast friends in the faith.

Then there were William Alexander and Everette Hill. They were two of our young people who, along with my daughters Taylor Ann and Sarah Page, caught the vision of what it means to be a Christian while you're putting down tile. William and Everette were the muscle of that team. As it turned out, these guys came on the trip because they were searching for meaning. They probably didn't expect to find it in the floor of that church. Both of them, during their semester breaks, went out to Colorado and help install floors out there. It all happened because, for some reason, they heard God's whisper to "get up and go" and serve the Lord in New Orleans. It's a God Thang!

Sometimes God provides the right person for a job that has to be done just so. A good example of that is Don Miller of Community Christian Church in Manchester, Missouri. During the most intense rebuilding work on Pastor Washington's church, Don showed up with forty-six volunteers. There was work for all them, and especially for Don. He described it this way:

At the beginning of the week, because I'd been down there so much and I can manage volunteers, Vance turned me loose and told me what had to be done and where to send workers. We broke our group up over five separate sites.

He gave me the job he didn't want anyone else to do: hang the new "security" doors on Greater New Jerusalem Missionary Baptist Church. I was instructed that they had to be secure, but not look like security doors. He

*said, "You're the only one I know who's good
enough to do this."*

*By Thursday night, we hadn't had time to do
the doors. So Vance took over and managed the
rest of the projects. I took another young man
from my church and we took all day and hung
the doors. We hung them in concrete block.
What a task it was because the block was
anything but level and square. But we got them
hung right.*

Alex Watkins, who is a member of Post Oak Baptist
Church in Russellville, Kentucky, came down to New
Orleans with the group from Berea Christian Church.
He wrote to share what happened with him spiritually
as he worked on Pastor's church:

*We were given the task of finishing the dry
wall of the choir loft of Greater New Jerusalem
Missionary Baptist Church in the Lower Ninth
Ward. Now the choir loft of this church was
actually in the rear of the sanctuary. You might
wonder why this has anything to do with the
story. This is where it all took place and my life
began to fall into place.*

*After the first couple days on the job, I
began to sense God was telling me something I
had never heard before. I remember sitting on
the ground working on the back-left corner of
the loft, trying to fix a beam so we could nail the
sheetrock into it. I can still see exactly what I
was doing when God began to talk to me. At
first, I wasn't sure what was actually
happening, but then I realized God was telling
me something much greater than I had ever*

imagined. That was the day. Greater New Jerusalem Missionary Baptist Church was the place. God was speaking. I was listening. And I acted.

That was the day I felt God calling me to something greater than I could have ever thought. He called me to be in mission with him and into a life of leading worship. I did not share this with anyone at the time because I wanted to make sure God was doing the talking and not me. I wanted to make sure I was actually following what he was saying and not doing something just because I wanted to do it.

The Sunday after I returned from New Orleans, I was approached by the head of the Minister of Music search committee. Our church had been without a music minister for a couple years. They were in the process of trying to find the right man. She asked me if I had given any thought to placing my resume before the committee. By January 1, 2009, Post Oak Baptist Church had called me to be the Minister of Music.

Working in New Orleans literally changed my life. I praise God for choosing me to be in mission with him and for wanting to use me to serve him. You never know what might happen on a mission trip. I always tell others when I speak that you never know what God has in store for you until you choose to follow him and listen when he speaks.

It hadn't been that long after we finished rebuilding the church when Pastor called me on a Sunday morning to tell me he had thirteen people to baptize that morning. The next day he called me back and said, "You know I made a mistake. It was only twelve because one of them came by letter."

That said to me there were twelve people who said "yes" to Jesus Christ in that old man's church. In light of those souls accepting Christ, the $37,000 we invested in rebuilding that church seemed like a pittance. It would have been pittance if only one person said "yes" to Jesus Christ. I have never doubted our decision to rebuild Greater Jerusalem Church since. Nor have I doubted any other decision I feel like God is leading me to make.

There was another aspect about Pastor's wide influence that I didn't recognize at first, but which turned out to be very significant. After we finished the church, we started to work on the fellowship building next door. It was a two-story structure with a number of small rooms that had to be rebuilt. During that process, whenever we needed drywall, lumber or other large construction supplies, Pastor would use his truck to pick up the materials. A volunteer with a list would ride with him to the lumberyard or the hardware store.

During one week of the reconstruction, a group from North Carolina was tearing out walls and reinstalling supports on the lower level. This required a number of trips to different suppliers. After several days of riding all over the Lower Ninth Ward, Mike Simpson, the volunteer assigned to purchase the materials, approached me and remarked that everywhere they went, the people they saw knew Pastor Washington.

"Riding down the street, people call his name and he waves," he said. "We go into the store and people come up and start talking to him. There's not a single place we went where somebody didn't recognize him. I think he's the best known man in the Lower Ninth Ward."

I realized from that comment the true extent of what God was doing through our mission work with Pastor and his church. Greater Jerusalem Church was pretty much the first church to be rebuilt in the Lower Ninth Ward after Hurricane Katrina, a place where there had been many, many small churches. Other churches have begun to return. I think the faith of Pastor in believing his church would be renewed has not only inspired his congregation and brought many others to it, but also had planted seeds of hope in a multitude of other Christians in the Lower Ninth Ward as well. The reconstruction of one church breathed life into a number of other congregations.

Oddly enough, ironically enough, the seeds of hope were not just planted in Christian folks. While we were working on the Greater Jerusalem Church there was a Muslim fellow, Lahouisine Belanouane, who watched what was happening. After watching the crew work, he came to Pastor Washington and asked, "How are you getting people to work on your place?" Pastor told him that he prayed. Mr. Belanouane said, "I do pray, five times a day." Pastor told him to keep praying.

About that time, I came driving up and we were introduced to one another. He retold me his story. He didn't say, "Nobody will help me because I'm a Muslim," but that was the feeling I got.

I went over and looked at this house. He had done a lot of work himself, but the outside needed painting and there were some other things that needed doing. I had a group of volunteers there from Denver, Colorado. I told them of the need and I also shared with them that Mr. Belanouane was a Muslim.

Their remark to me was, "Okay. Where does he

live?"

So we went over to his house and worked on it. They worked on it just as they had on every other project. I developed a wonderful, lasting relationship with him. When I think of our how volunteers helped him, I remember how Jesus was so willing to help the Canaanite women, the Roman centurion, Samaritans and Greeks. Critical presence is a tangible expression of God's love and therefore knows no boundaries.

Volunteers also worked on Pastor Washington's home.

This dynamic of real Christian love in action was expressed well by a member of Russellville Kentucky's Berea Christian Church, Jonathan Noe. He wrote:

I saw God in the story of the Good Samaritan being played out. Lots of people criticized and said the people of New Orleans didn't deserve help and some believed that they even deserved a wake up call. Be we as

Christians responded without question. We got up and we acted.

With Pastor and his congregation, there have been many moving experiences, a great many moments where we have seen God at work. One in particular I will never forget involved a fellowship meal we were having one night at the mission center. We came to that part of the evening where we ask the question, "Where did you see God today?"

Pastor's grandson stood up and began to tell us a story about two conversations between Pastor and his son—the grandson's father. He said, "I'll tell a story. My daddy told us that, when they were growing up, he resented my grandfather, Howard, because Howard would do stuff for other people. Daddy felt like he could do more for his own family if he didn't do stuff to help other people. Daddy specifically talked about the time Howard brought home a guy that was a drunk. He cleaned him up, fed him, gave him a place to sleep and just kind of let him hang at his home for a few days to let him get back on his feet. How Daddy resented that. He resented Howard for doing that." As it turned out, this resentful son was the very one who had told Pastor it was a waste of time to try to bring back the church after the hurricane.

Then the grandson began to describe the conversation that took place between his father and Howard after we had repaired the church. He related that Pastor's son said to him, "Daddy, all those years I almost hated you because you would help people. When we would say something to you, you would always say the Lord was going to pay you back for the things that you do. If it's good, he's going to pay you back good and if bad, you're going to get paid back bad.

I didn't believe you. When that church flooded, all I wanted you to do was just shut the doors and come home. I didn't think that you could ever put it back together. But you met this man, Brother Vance, and he brought in all these volunteers who did all this work. Today the church looks better than it's ever looked. God didn't just pay you back. He paid you back many times over."

Inspired by her many mission trips to Westside, North Carolina artist Janice Taylor created her first ever portrait, an image of Pastor Howard Washington.

As his grandson was telling that story, there were many tears shed by those sitting around the tables, and some of them were coming from Howard Washington's eyes.

Karen Zuver of Hiram Christian Church in Hiram, Ohio, added the final note to that story when she wrote me later and said:

> *Where did I see God? When the people whose homes you're working on come in to see what's being done or maybe when they come back with all their family and friends to show them with bright eyes and full, whole smiles. Or maybe when one of the sons of a family you're helping takes back all the things he said regarding, "Why would those people come down here to us?" Those are times when I've seen God.*

Once I was asked the question, has the whole Lower Ninth Ward community seen what happened to Howard and his church, the way God restored everything, perhaps even better than before the flood? I know that people compared Pastor to the biblical figure Job whose fortunes were restored after he lost everything. Folks have said God gave the church back to Pastor back better than it had been before the flood. Is the whole Lower Ninth Ward aware of what has happened to him and his church? I think the answer is "yes." In Howard, I think, the Lower Ninth Ward sees a man who always gave and gave and gave. I think they see God saying, "I'm not going to let you go away. I'm going to take care of you," and God being true to his word.

These experiences with Pastor not only reinforced my awareness of how the Spirit of God transforms our lives at the moment of critical presence. They also helped me to see how observing these God Thangs can have a great impact on others. This is directly behind the continued growth of Pastor's church, I believe, and also to a degree part of the reason for the resurgence of congregational rebuilding in the Lower Ninth Ward. I hope my readers will recognize that, in the previous chapter, we focused a lot on how our mission work transformed the lives of homeowners and other residents of the mission site. This chapter, which has dealt largely with the rebuilding of Pastor Washington's church, has focused more on the transformations brought about in our mission volunteers themselves. The God Thangs of Westside were evenly distributed between the helpers and the people who helped, which is the real essence, I think, of critical presence. I perceived that in a story that was shared with me by Jonathan Noe of Berea Christian Church in Russellville, Kentucky:

> We saw God right on the streets of New Orleans in a prayer circle. The first year we were down here, we were eating at Bubba Gump, and we received a phone call that a beloved member of one family was facing some medical concerns. We stepped outside that restaurant and had a prayer on the sidewalk. That evening during our meeting, Bro. Vance sensed something was wrong. He said, "I don't know what is wrong and I don't need to know what is wrong, but just know that it will be okay because God is in control." The test results came back fine and prayers were answered.

Bob Sieck also wrote something that helped me

remember God Thangs can happen to any of us, regardless of our station in life, theology, preconceptions or even our age

I have witnessed transformations particularly among some of the young persons our church has brought down to New Orleans. Seeing firsthand what people have been through and how they are coping has truly changed some of the young people's view of what matters and what commitment means.

By the time we finished actual work on the Greater Jerusalem Church buildings, I had a pretty clear understanding of how the Spirit of God reaches out and transforms people through the intersection of need and ability. What I didn't have yet was a name for it or a full theoretical framework to understand it. Those things were to come to me soon however as God led me to, of all places, the Dominican Republic.

Chapter 6

Not long ago I was asked if, during those years of rapid change and uncertainty at Westside, had there been points along the way when I thought Westside would close or its mission would become so unfocused as to become ineffectual? In the beginning, those were fears I had daily. In the beginning, I was always asking myself questions. How long can we stay open? Where will we find the resources to stay open? What sort of mission will Westside become? How will we be transformed over time? Into what sort of institution will we evolve?

Certainly, those questions continued throughout the life of the mission. We were always at a financial crossroads. We were always asking ourselves if we were truly who God was calling us to be, doing what God called us to do? Were we still able to be flexible enough so we could change as God called us to face new challenges in living out his commission? We kept asking this because it became clear just how important it was to be sensitive to the shifts in the mission field. Here is a principle that holds for Christians interested in serving Christ and others, regardless of whether we're talking about a mission site like Westside or the ministry of any local church: it's essential that we Christian servants talk to God on a daily basis. The needs of the community change and so the call of God upon us periodically also changes. Therefore, I think we have to be attuned to this reality and remain constantly flexible in our service.

The willingness to go where God sends you, to say "yes" to God's Spirit, is essential. I have perceived this truth throughout my ministry, but the significance of it came home most clearly to me early in 2009, when it seemed certain I was going to have to leave Westside for good.

Pat Burke, lay leader of Westside Christian Church, and Vance rejoice as the church's sanctuary nears completion.

This situation began to develop as we faced the looming reality that help from any outside institutional funding was coming to an end. We had a feeling of inevitability about this because we knew all along that day would come. There were no other apparent resources. None. As much as I would have liked to be a philanthropist, I couldn't. Just like everybody else, I had to make a living. I had already served Westside Christian Church as its pastor without a salary for four years.

I realized the only way Westside Mission Center stood any chance of going forward would be for me to move out of the picture and for the region to be able to design a way to do the work at Westside Mission Center with all-volunteer effort. While I was very skeptical that could be done, I knew I was going to be gone regardless. I was no longer going to be part of the Westside equation.

Once it seemed certain I was going to leave, I met with the Regional Board officially to make the final decisions. I put my relocation papers out and was in the process of being called to a church in Missouri. I had met with their search committee. They voted unanimously to call me as their pastor. I had met with their board. They voted unanimously to call me. I had traveled there and preached to the congregation and was waiting on the congregational vote to make it certain. It seemed quite clear I was going to be a resident of Missouri.

Then I had one final meeting with the Great River Region Board. From the beginning of my work at Westside, I had always been responsible to the board. The board was responsible for the creation of Westside. So I met with them to summarize my work at Westside. I gave an accounting of all my financial activities:

"This is how many houses we've built," and so on. Then I said goodbye and left. I preached my final sermon at Westside Christian Church on Sunday and then took a day off on Monday to meet with Michael Elmore. Michael was my regional pastor at the time, an understanding advisor and friend, and together we conducted an exit interview.

During the exit interview process something came up that required us to make a phone call to the regional office. When we did, we found out that the Great River Region Executive Committee had met and, without me knowing anything about it, voted to call me as a regional pastor in an effort to try to maintain Westside as a functional mission center. When they offered me the regional pastor position, without knowing any details of the job responsibilities or the details of the package whatever, I said "yes."

As I reflected later upon what had happened, I realized that, while the folks in Missouri wanted me there and I was certainly willing to go, there was another Power that wanted me at Westside. When I recognized the voice of God speaking to me, I realized I was being called to remain here in the Great River Region and continue empowering the vital work of Westside Mission.

This was a major God Thang. This is what I mean about being open to God's leading. Every time I try to "fly the plane", it crashes. When I shut up and listen to God the plane takes off and soars. Now I'm a regional pastor. If you look the normal requirements for a regional minister—or a regional pastor or a district minister, whatever title you want to put on it—the educational requirements are greater than my educational level. This goes for every aspect of the job. If you look at the traditional administrative requirements of the position, I don't fit the description. The thing is everybody forgot to tell God, "Brother Vance doesn't fit the mold of a regional pastor."

So I can say with no reservations that I am a regional pastor. I can also say this could only have happened because we got out of the way and let God speak and we listened as he spoke.

I tell this story as a way of saying that the same sort of dynamic happens in the lives of a great many people who volunteer. They end up reaching out to other people in their moment of desperate need—the moment of critical presence. As a result, everyone involved in the process is transformed. This doesn't just happen to those volunteers who came to New Orleans and worked through Westside. It also happens to people who volunteer in their own hometowns and never leave the city limits.

Young men from First Christian Church in Meridian, Mississippi, put the finishing touches on the Westside bunkhouse.

I've been asked, what happens to the volunteers who conduct this sort of ministry and have that critical presence experience? What happens to the people on the receiving end of this ministry when they receive help at the moment of critical presence?

As people prepare to enter into mission work, regardless of where it is—it could be in your local community—or whatever sort of mission it is—they ask themselves first of all, "Why are we doing this?" In fact, I have asked this question of literally thousands of volunteers: "Why are you here? Why are you doing what you're doing?" Assuming we are asking this question during the orientation period—which is at the beginning of the mission—the initial answer is almost always, "I came to help people. I came to do a good thing for somebody, to give something to somebody else."

But then we start working together. We start interacting with people who are in need. We form a relationship with the people we are helping. This happens in just a very short period of time, a short number of days. As this happens, the statement, "I came to help somebody," changes to, "I want to tell you what I'm getting out of this. I want to tell you what's happening to me and for me because I let Jesus work through me."

Carol Kees of Berea Christian Church in Russellville, Kentucky, captured the real essence of what it's like as a volunteer to become spiritually one with the people we are assisting. Her words, for me, are a wonderful bridge from the colonial mission viewpoint ("let's help those poor folks and be glad we're not them") to the critical presence viewpoint, ("this is my neighbor, whom I will love and serve"):

Like moving through stages of grief and death, these people whose lives were disrupted by Katrina are having to recover slowly. They are on a path that no one can understand unless they have been in their shoes. These people have lost everything they had, including peace of mind. They don't get to have the expectations of normalcy ever again because they fear that everything could just be gone again at any moment. Once you survive something as traumatic as they have, I've decided, you can never fully recover and move on.

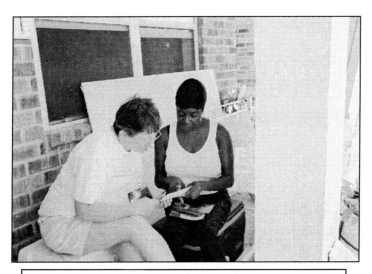

Dee Jones, right, shares photos of the demolition and rebuilding process with volunteer Claudia Colter.

It's a transforming experience to minister to people in such situations and to have them respond as a neighbor to your ministry. When we get "us" out of the way and let Christ work through us to help someone else, therein lies the actual transforming experience. In allowing Christ to work through me, I experience Christ.

I think one of the most compelling expressions of the distinction between colonial mission work and critical presence mission work has been expressed by Tom Sikes. Along with a group of medical first responders, Tom and the others were on hand when a second team arrived—a team that had not experienced the human suffering that resulted from the Katrina, but clearly assumed they understood the situation and what needed to be done:

A group made up of the medical staff from a top tier medical school came down. They arrived late one night. By then we were all very tired, just exhausted. We were excited to pass the baton to them. They walked into the gymnasium and we noticed that they were taking it all in. They were very skilled, very smart, and eager to help. But it seemed they were on guard.

The head physician reached out his hand to our doctor. He said his name and reeled off his credentials. Our doctor said, "I am Dr. Randy Nance. And I am a human being." It was stunning. The well-healed doctor was taken aback and it spoke volumes.

We found ourselves at odds right away with this new team from the medical school as they began to show us how we had not properly set up the clinic. If they had only seen the first days of this storm and how you had to do what you could with what you had. Well, with a mixture of resentment and grace, we worked together.

Days later, as they began to get to know

their new patients and what we had all been through, the new team softened and better understood the context of serving on the front lines of Katrina. We understood that God was still moving in our midst. The medical school team took the clinic to the next level. We all had to realize it wasn't "our turf" or "their turf." It was God's turf, where all were offered hope and healing.

And I need to add another concept here that is very important in understanding the essence of helping people, a concept necessary for understanding the essence of critical presence itself. As I begin to experience the presence of Christ in my mission work, I begin to move away from acting in a "colonial" fashion. Colonial mission work is when I reach out to help someone strictly the way I want to do. I move away from colonialism when I truly begin to grasp and care about what's important to that person. My desire to help begins to coincide with the actual need of the person I'm helping. In my view, that's becoming one with Christ and becoming one with the person who needs my help. In my view, that is really what loving my neighbor means.

The longer I worked at Westside, putting volunteers from all over into the New Orleans communities where they were so desperately needed, the more I understood: *The dynamic of true service is loving your neighbor in such a way that Christ could work through you and both of you would be transformed.* What I did not know as I was learning this truth was that, with the leadership of the Spirit, I was about to be given a name for this concept. I was about to receive a theoretical framework that would fully allow me to understand this process we've come to call critical presence. In retrospect, I realize that everything in my ministry had been preparing me for this discovery.

Ray Foxworth and the miraculously restored charcoal portrait of his father.

As I've related in the first chapter, I've been in the

ministry for a number of years. The first part of my ministry was as a parish pastor, the minister of a local congregation. As with all pastoral ministries, there was the preaching experience, there was the nurture experience and there was some degree of evangelism or outreach. All of these things in the church experience are essential and of course, I celebrate those ministries. When I came to Westside, though, I began to see what happens when we truly do allow God to work through us and we help people.

2009 mission workers from Tucson and Phoenix Arizona pose for a photo. Like many of the more than 4000 volunteers who came to Westside to help rebuild New Orleans, the majority of these workers made multiple trips.

Let me confess that, when I first came to Westside, I had a colonial attitude. I say that because I personally had an extensive construction background before I came to the ministry. This area to which I was called was devastated—90,000 houses destroyed—and it was easy for me to jump in and take volunteers to go out and clean up and fix up and get people back in their houses. I'm not taking away from that because there is a tremendous amount of need for that here and there will be for many more years.

Quickly, though, something began to happen to change my attitude. I found myself entering into profound relationships with all sort of people who were doing the rebuilding. All sorts of people who came down here were living out their version of helping people. I began to witness the dynamic I've tried so hard to describe: people helping other people in such a way that those they assisted could heal—not only physically, but mentally, emotionally and spiritually. I realized it meant taking the time to become part of that other person's life, being willing to befriend them, being open to having a relationship with them and being able to understand what was going on in their lives. And I knew in my heart-of-heart that, when we worked that way to help others, we were doing the right thing. It was changing everyone who was involved.

Here was a phenomenon I recognized, a phenomenon I participated in regularly. It was sort of like the "name of the animals" story in the second chapter of Genesis: the creature was there and I recognized—I just didn't have a name for it.

Tom Russell described this phenomenon so well as he was writing about the change that happens both to volunteers and the people they assist.

I have been with people who have experienced great loss and they find peace especially when others come to help. Yet somehow, God always ministers to me more than I can ever minister to others when I put *myself into mission work. My wife gave me a very special piece of art that has this inscribed, "Christian Mission Begins When We Are Physically Present To Those In Need". I believe this is **the purpose** God has given me. And God fills this purpose so full of gifts and rewards that I can't stop serving in this work. I think that most of my mission partners feel this too.*

Then, as I was recognizing and rejoicing in all the miraculous transformation I was seeing—but still not having a full theoretic framework or a name for it—another God Thang happened. I was invited to go to the Dominican Republic and participate in MMI (Ministries and Mission Interpreters) Training. MMI interpreters, according to the way they are officially described by our denomination are:

. . . individuals passionate about mission and trained to convey the stories of mission and educate people in local churches about the work of mission around the world. MMIs represent their region (Disciples), conference (UCC) or constituency group. Currently there are fully trained and equipped MMIs actively interpreting in about two-thirds of our Conferences and Regions across the country.

The interpreters are the extended staff of Global Ministries, joining our partners in the US and across the world. The purpose is to create a ripple effect of raising awareness and passion for mission in the local church by training others to tell the stories and use our resources. The MMI group remains closely networked to each other through listserves, mailings, and regular communiqués. They are available to speak, present workshops, arrange for missionary visits, provide displays and encourage ideas for mission events.

My invitation to attend this training did not come out of the blue. Quite a few of our Disciples regional ministers were taken to Haiti and the Dominican Republic in 2009 by David Vargas, of our Overseas Mission. One of those regional ministers was our own Barb Jones. She returned from this event having been quite impacted and felt strongly that the Great River Region should become a global mission partner.

Many of the other regions chose to partner with Haiti. Of course, this was before the January 10, 2010 earthquake and we had no idea what was going to happen. The need in Haiti, even before that disaster, was great.

Barb, however, saw real similarities between the people and the culture of the Dominican Republic and the people and culture of Mississippi, Arkansas and Louisiana. Some of those similarities have to do with agricultural. Some are cultural. New Orleans is an international city. So many of the people who have ended up in this Crescent City area are from that part of the world. There are so many people here of French and Spanish descent, and there are French and Spanish people in the Dominican Republic as well.

When Barb came back, she was on fire with what she had experienced and the inspiration it gave her. She asked me to go down and just become acquainted with the people of the Dominican Republic so we could ask the right question to begin the process of creating an agreement to partner with them.

So, after my MMI training, I went to the Dominican

Republic without really knowing what to expect. I didn't have a clue that the experience was in effect going to focus and explain everything God had been teaching me about mission and ministry. During my MMI training, I heard Bob Schebeck of Disciples Global Ministries stand up and say, "True mission is about meeting people at their point of deepest need." And then he did what I've always aspired to do in my own ministry. He backed up his statement with scripture. He said, "Jesus did it this way and if Jesus did it this way, that's how it should be done."

If you want to talk about an epiphany or an "aha moment," that was my aha moment. It felt so much like standing up and shouting, "Yes, that's what I've been feeling!"

Of course, this is not a reflection on anyone else's theology of ministry. I'm certainly not saying that somebody is doing it right or and someone else is doing it wrong. I'm saying that I heard Bob say out loud in a theoretical way what I already knew about mission in the depths of my heart. He expressed the notion of critical presence in clear theological language, in perfectly accessible spiritual terms. Not only was I hearing a confirmation of what I already knew, but it was the beginning of an experience that was to complete my total transformation.

I made the trip to the Dominican Republic with folks from the Oklahoma region. People from that region had already been going there for the previous two or three years. This is a mission event that has gained tremendous importance for the Oklahoma region. We had the opportunity to experience *Caminata*, which translates as "children walking".

Children from the Lower Ninth Ward begin a football game with kids from Crown Heights Christian Church in Oklahoma City. In the foreground on the bicycle is Dee Jones's grandson.

Following this, I had the opportunity to meet with a group of Dominican evangelical pastors. Together we began to explore how we might engage in some sort of mutual mission work. As I write, we haven't decided yet how to proceed with this shared ministry because we're working through the discernment process. This helps us to avoid the colonial approach I described above. Together, we who are doing the mission work will decide with our local partners and the people we will be assisting just what sort of work needs to be done. We're being guided through this with the help of Felix Ortiz, who is the Global Ministries Area Executive for Latin America and the Caribbean. Specifically, he is to help us determine the critical presence needs we are being called to address.

It looks as if we're going to have the opportunity to

partner with about forty Dominican evangelical churches. For me the long-term goal is to form partnerships between churches in the Great River Region and sister churches in the Dominican Republic. In this way, we can share ministry that will not only enhance and benefit the Dominican Republic, but that will enhance and benefit the Great River congregations as well. To me this is the embodiment of the concept of the true Christian family: *brothers and sisters in Christ, serving (BASICS)* and working with each other.

I have to say that, after I finished going through the MMI training and traveled down to the Dominican Republic, I saw some of the most dedicated, on-fire Christian spiritual presences I have ever seen in my life. The Dominican Christians I encountered are poor in one way and wealthy in another way—in a way that really counts.

Nobody, in my opinion, should live in a house with a dirt floor, but many of those I met do. I saw a woman living in a hut—a shack, a shanty, whatever you want to call it—with a dirt floor, but she was hard at work sweeping it to keep it as clean as possible. Her children were lying there on the floor, studying their schoolbooks. She was making sure they learned their lessons. She was determined they were going to have a better life than she had.

In the Dominican Republic, you talk to people like her and you see a presence, a Holy Spirit within them that is so rare in our world today. This is the same Spirit, though, that I witnessed in so many people we worked with in New Orleans, Louisiana. The recognition of this similarity was an eye-opening experience. It said to me, "We've got to do something to help these people." The world is a hurting world. Our "slice of the pie" is found in helping others, in sharing the love of Christ with them.

Someone might ask, "how does Christ want us to love one another?" In the Gospel of Luke, when the lawyer asked, "Who is my neighbor," Jesus responded by telling the Parable of the Good Samaritan.

He said first, "You know the law."

I think that's very important. It reminds us of something we all really know already. We know that we're supposed to love everybody. The reality is we love the people we want to love, or who love us, while we struggle with loving other people.

An event happened on April 18, 2010 that drove home to me the great distinction between the reality of typical human behavior and the way Christ calls us to love one another. Perhaps part of the reason this had such an impact on me was because it happened on a Sunday. As it was reported in the national media, there was a homeless man from Guatemala who was living in New York. His name was Hugo Alfredo Tale-Yax. He had been living and working in the United States for six years before the economic downturn. He lost his job and then his home.

He was out on the streets of New York City at 6 a.m. that Sunday morning and saw a mugger attempting to rob a woman. Hugo intervened and stopped the mugger from hurting the woman. In the process though, he was stabbed multiple times. He walked a short way down the street and fell on the sidewalk. Videos of him lying there were taken for over an hour. They showed many people coming by to look at him, though no one did anything to help him. One fellow even took a picture of him and then just walked off. Finally, someone called the paramedics. By the time they arrived, Hugo had died.

The news reports referred to Hugo as "a good

Samaritan." That is a perfect parallel of the gospel story. Like the Samaritan in Luke, Hugo took great personal risks to help a stranger. As I listened to the reports and the comments of experts of why something like this could happen in this desensitized age of ours, suddenly it struck me: this was what Christ was talking about when he said, "You know who your neighbor is. Go and do likewise.'"

Is that a radical example? Yes, it is absolutely a radical example. But having said that, I think we must acknowledge we have reached the point in our society where we have become willing to accept injustice. We have accepted all sorts of lawlessness. We have accepted a life without spirituality. This is the world we live in today, and I'm not telling anyone anything they don't already know. In my view, the world is the way it is because we have quit living out that relationship that Christ calls us to. We have been called to live a Christ-like life.

To be sure, under the best circumstances, we would never fully get there. There was only one perfect one. We all know that. We aren't perfect and we can't heal every situation. But when it reaches the point that we see something like what happened to a real-life "good Samaritan" like Hugo Alfredo Tale-Yax, stabbed and lying on the sidewalk, dying while scores of people walked by him doing nothing to assist him, we can no longer simply remain complacent and say, "Well, that's the way the world is today." If we do, you and I are just as much at fault as the mugger who stabbed him. Thankfully, we don't have to accept the brokenness of the world.

A great friend and supporter of our work at Westside, Keith Strain, touched on the distinction between the society we live in and society Christ calls us to build. When I read his words, I was most grateful for the affirmation I felt:

> *In part, I continue to come to Westside and participate in the rebuilding work because I realize how quickly the focus of American culture shifts. People in great need very quickly become the forgotten. I have learned from working in New Orleans that problems are always far more complex than we first imagine and the easy answers "armchair quarterbacks" make, do not come close to the reality being lived out by people. Poverty is one of those issues that is so blithely talked about by those not living it.*
>
> *The deeper lesson I have learned from my brother, Vance, is that God is working in all things for good. I know I've read that somewhere, but in working with and for Vance, I began to see its reality.*
>
> *I have learned that no great movement ever happens until one person has a clear vision that they can articulate and a passion to make the vision a reality.*
>
> *Brother Vance is that visionary and his passion continues to ignite our compassion.*

My colleague Michael Elmore in his essay, *What I Learned From Disaster Response,* talks about how the ministry of critical presence goes even further in tearing down all the walls that divide us:

> *I have learned that when we are serving God by serving others all our differences are overcome. I do not recall anyone asking any*

volunteer, *"Are you a conservative or liberal, are you Republican or Democratic, are you straight or homosexual?" When we focus on what is essential, service of God by serving others, the things that divide us are overcome. We don't waste time over silly theological issues that really, in the long term do not matter. I heard someplace "In essentials unity, in non-essentials tolerance, in all things love."*

I have learned that our response to Katrina, Rita, Gustav and Ike has given us a model of how we can transform our denomination and our congregations. When [our denomination's] general units and regions see their mission as serving the local congregations and when we work with each other and with the local church to empower them we will all be transformed. We have to give up our desire to build ourselves up and [instead] work with each other to transform and build up the local congregation which is where ministry and mission happens

As Alan Roxburgh is so fond of saying, "The future of God is among the people of God." Who are the people of God? They are the ordinary people sitting beside us every Sunday in some local congregation. There is God's future.

Two servants of God, Pastor Washington and Bro. Vance celebrate communion.

The experiences of Westside Mission Center have taught us that working for our Lord brings about positive change, the sort of transformation we could honestly describe, as our Savior did, as "the Kingdom of God". In the final chapter, we're going to talk about how local congregations can develop ministries of critical presence, so that churches and individuals everywhere can experience the transforming power of Christ.

Chapter 7

It's always jarring to me when I hear people say, "I can't figure out God's will for my life." To me that statement sounds like a way of complicating things spiritually for ourselves, perhaps even a way to avoid recognizing how God is already at work in our lives. I'm reminded of the great Christian author Leslie D. Weatherhead, who begins his book, *How Can I Find God*, by saying that the real question is, "Why won't I let God find me?"

So often, it seems to me we can't accept the fact that spirituality is really quite simple. For me, this begins with interpreting the scriptures. When we pick up God's word and start reading—regardless of the translation—if we're in the right place spiritually, we don't have to be hindered by the complexity of the Bible. Even if we're not Bible scholars, still we can understand that God's Word has direct, intentional meaning for us.

Take the gospels, for instance. So often Jesus made simple, clear statements that anyone can apprehend. He said things like, "Love God with all your heart, your soul, your mind and your strength. Love your neighbor as you love yourself." What part of that is difficult to understand?

So what about God's will and our part in it? If you accept the premise that Almighty God made you (and I do; he is the Creator after all), then the Creator made you, as me, with a certain number of talents. It seems clear to me that this is part of what Jesus is talking about when he tells parables about talents. And in those parables, the dynamic is obvious and simple. We are told we must use the talents we have been given, or we will lose them.

Now consider the person who claims not to know God's will for his or her life. It seems to me God is asking that person, "Hey, friend, about that talent—or skill, or ability or vision—I gave you, are you going to use it or are you going to squander it?" In that light, it's really disingenuous for any of us to say, "I just can't figure out God's will for me."

Suppose, from this perspective, we want to discover what God's will for us is. The first thing we need to do is look at the talents we've been given. Each of us should look at the God-given abilities we possess. And then the next thing we need to do is ask, "Since I recognize I have this ability, how can I match it up to some unmet need that is out there?" We look at the community where we live and ask, "Is there a need in my community for the talent that I have?"

Let me go out on a limb and challenge any reader: I guarantee you can match the talent God gave you to a need in your local community. The principle at work here is this: *God's will is found at the intersection of your talent and the needs of the community in which you live.*

I have made that statement repeatedly in my work at Westside. Someone pointed out the other day that I always make this sort of "cross sign" when I say that and I realized I have gotten in the habit of doing that. I'm trying to show the up-standard, the vertical line of the cross, as your talent. One of the reasons I like that as an illustration is because, when you start out, you may perceive your talent to be diminutive—small or short. But as you put your abilities to use, as you exercise those "talent muscles" much as you would exercise any other muscles, your talent grows. Your skills, abilities and vision expand dramatically and become a lot more powerful. This is much like what the Apostle Paul wrote in I Corinthians, we start off drinking milk, but as we mature, our diet is transformed to that of an adult. So as servants of Christ we get to a place where we can say, "I'm not on milk any more. It's time to eat some meat. It's time to take the talent God has given me, now that I can see what it is, and put it to its proper use." Candidly, that's the way to take your talent and make it grow. That how God wants our talents to be used.

There comes a point when your maturing talent meets the horizontal piece: human need, the needs of your community. In my experience, as we work to discover our abilities, God's Spirit invariably leads us to a place where those talents can be used. Yes, sometimes it's also the case we find ourselves at a point of real need and in responding we discover abilities we didn't know we possessed. The key is to be willing, to be open to the Spirit's leading.

What is true for individuals is likewise true for churches. As a congregation, I think it's important for the members of a church fellowship to work together in order to discover what abilities and interests are within the church. My experience is that the members of a church are almost always surprised to find out who in the church has a certain talent or interest. I've also found that working as a church fellowship within the community at large often has several significant results: it empowers the individuals involved; it increases the camaraderie of the church, and it builds the spirituality of the congregation—people get closer to the Lord. It also has the added benefit of speaking to the community as a whole, of saying, "This is what we are about: taking the gifts God has given us and reaching out to those in need in our midst."

Once I made a statement like that and someone expressed the belief that only strong, growing churches are capable of reaching out into the community with this sort of ministry. In the course of the discussion that followed, I was asked if it's possible for a congregation to do mission within its community when the church itself is declining or dying. This is a tremendously important question, the short answer to which is "yes." The heart of this chapter, in fact, is devoted to understanding how any church, regardless of the level of its vitality, can reach out to its community. Since we know that, as a result of the process, God's Spirit moves through the congregation with transforming power, we could say that *declining or dying churches are the very ones who most need to engage in this sort of mission, that they too might experience Christ's transforming power.*

To be sure, the degree of life in a church has an impact on how willing it is to enter into mission. Dormant churches often are reluctant to even consider engaging in this sort of ministry. This is because they believe it will be impossible for their fellowship to recruit a critical mass of people willing to make a commitment to mission. Despite this belief, however, the process boils down to something quite simple: someone within the congregation—and that someone might be the pastor, a lay leader, the chairman of the outreach committee, the chairman of the board—but somebody in the congregation sits down and asks the basic question, "Why does this church exist?" And a second question that automatically follows, regardless of the answer to the first question, is, "How do we live out our purpose for existing?"

At this point, it's important to come back to John 3:16, a verse spoken by Jesus that virtually every Christian knows by heart: "God so loved the world he gave his only son, that everyone who believes in him might not perish, but have everlasting life." If we had any doubt about the extent of God's love, all we have to do is consider his sacrifice as described in that passage. John 3:16 tells us a lot about how love is meant to be expressed. For our Lord, love implies action.

We know also that Christ tells us to love our neighbors as we love ourselves. Suppose instead of the lawyer's question ("Who is my neighbor?"), we ask the question, "What does it mean to love my neighbor?" If we do, we recognize immediately that love is not a passive thing but an active thing. Thus, we can conclude that, as those who bear the name of Christ, we exist and are gathered into congregations because of Christ's sacrificial love; and we exist in order to express Christ's love through our actions.

So how do we live out our Christian purpose? That question focuses us back on our own locality and the needs we observe in our community. As we consider the needs around us, we ask, "Okay, who in the church has the talent to meet those needs?"

Nobody gets off the hook. Everyone in the congregation in one way or another can participate in mission. The majority of members have some talent they can share, regardless of whether or not they have had the opportunity or inducement to use it. Apart from those in the fellowship with the necessary talents, there are also people in the church who have the resources to underwrite the work of those who are willing to put their talents to work. Then there are people I call the "prayer warriors." Here are three essential groups in your church: those who do the work, those who send

145

the workers and those who pray for the workers. From this perspective, everybody in the church can be a part of any need, of any mission the church decides to fulfill.

I'll come back to a fuller discussion of this process below, but first I'd like to make an essential spiritual observation. What I'm describing here is literally finding and following God's will for us as individuals and as congregations. And I have learned that *living out God's will results in the renewal of our spiritual lives*—again, both as individuals and as congregations.

I read once that we are all created with the need to search for the meaning of life. As we live out that quest, there comes a moment for each of us in which we recognize the need for closeness with a power that is greater than ourselves. When we minister to others at the moment of critical presence, we aren't just *talking* about Jesus, we are *doing* Jesus. Inevitably, that changes us. It creates within us a sense of, "I'm fulfilling God's intention for me. I know I can do this because I was meant and made to do it. I know that I am a living part of something that is greater than I am by myself. In fact I realize that, through my actions, I have become the body of Jesus Christ ministering in love to the world." These are bold statements to be sure, but I have seen the validity and power of them lived out dozens, even hundreds of times.

A wonderful example that comes to mind involves one of the groups I mentioned from Wabash College. At Wabash College, there's a fellow by the name of Dr. John Bayer who teaches religion. On one occasion, John came with a group from Wabash who brought with them five or six exchange students from China— communist China. And all of these young men were by their own definition atheists. Each night the group was there, we did our famous session: "Where did you see God today?" These young men sat through that session quietly every night—until the final night. I was surprised on that occasion to see one of the most adamant of the atheists raised his hand. I called on him. He said, "I still do not believe that there is a God. But if there is a God, I saw him today." And then he related to us a God experience. That is a profound change in someone as a result of being willing to be exposed to this experience.

The mission volunteers and the residents they helped saw God at work every day.

Dave Lunsford from First Christian Church in Crawfordsville, Indiana, was present during that experience. I particularly enjoyed his account of it:

> *During the evening talk session, the young man from China stood up among the forty-five*

*other men and said, "I am not of the faith that
the rest of you claim, but I have seen and felt
something here the last few days that I have not
felt before. I don't understand everything, but
this is something I need to explore."*

*My recollection is that Brother Vance said,
"Young man, I admire your courage and
welcome your comment. To have the courage
you have exhibited by standing up and telling a
group of men from a different country who have
a different faith says a great deal about your
heart. Many people who profess to be
Christians do not have the courage to do what
you just did. You have my admiration, and I
hope that you will return sometime in the future.
You will always find two things when you come
here. First will be respect. The second will be
love, because if you do not, then we are truly
denying that we are what we profess to be,
namely Christians." I thought Vance captured
that moment perfectly.*

Another person who comes to mind as we talk
about this sort of transformation is Don Miller. I
remember Don from early on in the Westside process.
He's a fellow from St. Louis. Don is a contractor and
someone who was actively involved as a youth sponsor.
When Don came down he was so impacted, and I don't
think this is an overstatement, it radically changed his
life. Otherwise, I would suspect he would not have
come back to Westside to do mission work so many
times.

In fact, Don and his first mission group from
Manchester, Missouri, were not supposed to come to
New Orleans at all. Their arrival was a major God

Thang. As Don described it earlier in the book, his youth group was supposed to be in Lincoln, Nebraska, helping to build a brand new church. A day or two before they were supposed to leave, the church build was canceled. ODV did not have a backup plan. They didn't have any place for this group to go. By default, this group ended up at Westside. Don had been and continues to work with the youth in his church, but he's also a fulltime contractor. So he came down to New Orleans and worked with his group that week. They worked on the mission center itself. I could tell when he left that he had been very impacted by the mission to be done in New Orleans. Soon he came back with another group, and then with another group, and another group. In five years he's came down seventeen times—only twice by himself. He almost always brought an enthusiastic, motivated group. Eventually he brought down 220 volunteers. His transformation has clearly motivated many others. A wonderful story about him was printed in an issue of *Disciple World* magazine in 2007.

Don also has enrolled in the licensed ministry or commissioned ministry training in the Mid-America Region. Early on, he told me he was searching for God's call in his life. His awareness of that call has grown and developed, so that recently he shared with me that he knows he is called to do ministry. He feels very confident that because of his construction background, God is going to use that talent in some way as a part of his ministry. To me this is the epitome of God calling someone and that person responding to God's will: a man called to the ministry, knowing that the Lord will utilize his talents in the field of construction, but also prepared to go wherever he is sent and minister in whatever way he is called.

Here's someone who's had a transforming experience and has a clear understanding God's will. But what I like best is Don's comment on his work at Westside and on God's call:

"It wasn't like I could pick and choose—it just happened that way." In my experience, this is a person who has felt and responded to the Lord's claim upon his life.

Another fellow in whom I witnessed this sort of transformation is Francis Tileson from Frankfort, Kentucky. Francis came down first with a group of six mission trip folks from Frankfort sent to Westside by the Division of Homeland Missions (DHM). The group came down and worked a week and left that Saturday to go back to Frankfort. That very Saturday night my phone rang. Francis was calling. He told me that I needed him, that I needed him to come back to work and to help us in our mission.

Francis is a very talented "construction dude," which is what he likes to be called. He came back and stayed for a week or so. He went back to Frankfort, then a little later on he came back a third time. On that occasion, he stayed for four months. For 120 days, he just stopped his life at his home and stayed at Westside and helped us to finish building the bunkhouse. Francis also helped us to complete the sanctuary. He helped us to rebuild the Greater New Jerusalem Missionary Baptist Church. Watching Francis grow in his ability and understanding of mission as well as growing as a deeply spiritual individual was not only a transforming experience for him but a transforming experience for me as well.

Tom Sikes, Pastor of Meridian First Christian, wrote me about a fellow in his congregation who was impacted in a very similar way:

Ed Owen helped lead all of our teams. He loves to work in the midst of chaos and let God do what God does. He's a contractor by trade. Ed brought materials and tools and, together with Brother Vance, he showed an incredible passion for fixing things, for bring hope to people without saying a word. Ed is all about action—and the faster the better. He caught the vision to serve. He became a licensed pastor through our church in order to help with first responders, and to help us become all the more a missional church.

At this point let's turn to a discussion of how this wonderful, transforming dynamic can be experienced in any willing congregation, by any Christian who is open to serving. The first thing, the major understanding I want to share with every church and Christian who has an interest in this, is that Christ has already pointed the way for us. When we turn to the scriptures to see how the Lord ministered, you see the very dynamic we've been talking about. He reached out to people with his gifts—healing, teaching, preaching, praying—just at the moment people needed those things the most. Christ ministered at the moment of critical presence. So let's mimic what he did. Research all the stories in the Bible where Christ helped somebody, you come back to this very simple notion: find a need you are capable of addressing and fill it. From the beginning of my ministry, I have taught that the secret to experiencing God, to being transformed and transforming others on behalf of the Lord is to find a need and fill it. I believe Christ shows us that very thing through his ministry.

As a preface to this discussion, let me say that

throughout this chapter I will occasionally digress in order to explain and expand upon some of the ideas and processes we're going to examine. To help clarify my approach in a simple way, you'll find in the addendum an outline that spells out the process I've detailed below.

Of course, it's only fair to express what our vision is—that is, the vision of people who understand the Gospel as I do; people who want to involve our congregations fully in meaningful mission work. Our vision is that we have been given the responsibility of carrying the Good News of the Gospel of Jesus Christ into the world and we have been called to do it through mission, through outreach.

From this perspective, if I was given the opportunity to come into a congregation and work toward building this sort of ministry, the first thing I would want to do is meet with the outreach committee (which in your church may be called the "social outreach," "community action," "local missions," or a host of other names). The reason I tend to start with the outreach committee is because the head of that particular group is often one of the people in the fellowship who is most interested in reaching out to the community. I would observe that, in a great many churches, committees are headed by people who have accepted their leadership role from a sense of obligation or duty rather than out of love for the sort of ministry the committee performs. Outreach committees, on the other hand, are often an exception to that. Many times the outreach chair really wanted that assignment, or was sought out by the church's leaders as a result of prayerful consideration.

I'd like to add just a word about the process of selecting committee chairs. As I mentioned, in many cases a chair's only real qualification to head the committee for which they have accepted responsibility is that she or he was willing to take the job. I'm not saying that's bad. Willingness to serve is extremely important. We've all witnessed people who take on jobs in the church because no one else would, and those individuals end up doing spectacular, creative work for the Lord. On the other hand, I think it's important to lift up the notion of a "prayer search." The prayer search is when the nominating committee or those leaders who are responsible for selecting lay leaders within the fellowship begin by committing themselves to praying together. In prayer, they ask God for insight into who within the congregation is the very best person to hold a particular job. Of course, this is only the first part of the process. The committee should go on to identify the talents of potential nominees and deliberate together. While many congregations do not employ the prayer search as a tool for determining committee leaders, my personal belief is that it should always be part of the process and indeed should be the first step to be taken.

Back to the discussion of developing a mission ministry, when I go into a church as a regional pastor I want to work with the outreach leaders. They are normally the first people I contact. In my initial conversation, I want to find out whether or not the congregation has a mission statement. I want to know whether or not the church has an understanding, a vision of where it's trying to go. If there is a mission statement in place, then we can immediately move to start identifying the talents of the chair and others interested in outreach. If the church doesn't have a vision, however, then we must begin to probe to discover the congregation's vision: what is your purpose as God's people and how do you express that purpose?

So how do I help a church discover its vision? I start with a simple process of asking the question, "Where are you trying to go? What are you trying to accomplish as a church of faithful Christians?"

I ask the outreach leaders of the congregation to express the spiritual identity of the church, to tell me what the church is doing as an expression of its Christian witness. In this part of the process, I find myself saying, "Let's look at where you are right now and in light of what you've said you're trying to accomplish. Based on where you are and where you've indicated you want to go, where will the church be in the process of that journey five years from today?"

As a general rule members of a congregation respond both in a positive and a negative way. The positive aspect is that virtually every church and every Christian wants to see dynamic change happen. They love the idea of transformation happening in their midst. At the very same time, there is also almost always a negative response that comes from self-doubt. Folks say, "I just don't have the talents to do real mission work."

When I encounter that inevitable "can't do" response, I immediately try to create an atmosphere in which that attitude is destroyed. I don't try to talk people out of their feelings. Instead, I start asking questions designed to discover where their passions for Christian service lie. Once people start dreaming about what they'd really like to do to serve the Lord, their doubts begin to fade. One person's passion may be building houses. Another may just really get passionate about hospital visits or nursing home visits or working with kids. There are so many different arenas in which we can work. And when the moment comes that their passion for service is expressed, I know we've found the "hot button" that enables those doubters to begin to dream, to begin to understand that they have everything necessary to do real mission.

Continuing with the process, after that first discussion with the outreach chair, it's time to start meeting with other church leaders. If possible, I'm going to meet with either the board chair, the pastor and the various committee heads, making certain to include the outreach and the evangelism chairs. The reason I'm saying "various" is because different congregations have different names for their committees. Plus there is a fair degree of overlap. In some places, it's the chair of outreach I need to deal with. In some places, it's the chair of evangelism. There are times you need both those people. I have to know how a congregation assigns responsibility for its various ministries.

When I meet with a board chairperson, the first thing I want to do is find out the passion and vision of that person. I try to find that out saying, "Share your vision with me." What is truly more important than a vision is that leader's attitude. Is the attitude, "We're growing and we need to do better"? Is the attitude, "We're dying and we're just posturing as we wait around for the funeral"? Once I get a feeling for the key lay leader's vision, I know whether I can work with that person or whether I've got to institute the "lead, follow or get out of the way" policy.

If I go into a church and I just meet total resistance from somebody, I do not waste my energy trying to change total resistance. Instead, I adopt the attitude: "You know who I am and you know what I'm trying to do. If you want to lead that effort, that's fine. If you don't want to lead it, but you're willing to be a part of it, that's the follow side and that's fine. And it's also fine if all you want to do is to come to church on Sunday and listen to the sermon." That's the "get out of the way" choice. So lead, follow or get out of the way. We're going to go forward and serve Christ no matter what your part in it is.

Once I was asked if I had ever come to a church that publicly professed a desire to do mission, but actually didn't have any real intention of getting involved in outreach. I was asked if I was exasperated when I encounter churches like that. I was asked if I felt like just giving up on them.

I have two responses to those questions. First is an observation. I'm not saying this is the norm, but there are a good many churches who say they have the desire to serve Christ without really possessing the impetus for real mission. It's important for members of these churches to understand there is a difference between just dreaming about doing mission—wishing thinking—and actually having a vision. We may wish we were going to do something, but until we come up with a written plan and do something concrete to implement it, it's just a dream. A lot of churches are at that wishful thinking place; a lot of Christians in churches are there in that place.

The second comment has to do with my own response. I'm human. Do I ever want to throw my hands up? Yeah. Then I go to bed at night and God kind of works on me a little bit and I get up the next morning and try to find another door to go to the same place. I guess that's my way of saying I don't give up on congregations just because they aren't past the wishful thinking place.

Back to the process, after meeting with the various

leaders, I try to get contact information for all members of the church. Part of the concept under which I operate is that the first thing we do is identify the leadership of the congregation. Then we identify committee members. Then whatever we do goes through a well-defined process. You've got administration. You've got committees. You've got committee members. Then you got a board and then you've got the general congregation. The idea is you work through all the proper steps in order to create an outreach program. As our Lord pointed out when John didn't want to baptize him, it's necessary to "fulfill all righteousness." When we work through all the steps necessary to establish the outreach program, no one can say that we have circumvented the rules or failed to get proper permission for this ministry—which is important because it's going to change the church.

The other good result of working through the process fully with the congregation is the indirect educational result. I think one of the biggest mistakes we make is in not teaching people within the church about what we're doing, why we're doing it and what we expect the result to be. We don't educate the congregation. Members know we've got an outreach program. They know we've got a mission. Still, they don't fully understand it.

My next meeting is an individual session with the outreach chair. In a conversational process during this meeting, I will try to identify first her or his vision for mission. Second, I want to know from the viewpoint of that person what level of enthusiasm and commitment is possessed by the overall leadership of the church. That is, I want to know if the outreach chair believes the church is behind him or her. Of course, I also want to know the level of the outreach person's commitment.

There are times when other people also participate in this meeting with the outreach chair. For instance, recently I was at a church in Jonesboro, Arkansas, to meet with the outreach chair. That individual has a close, personal relationship with the board chair and with a couple others, all of whom are already turned on to what we're doing. Because they were "where I wanted them to be," I brought them into that initial meeting.

When I'm able to have the leaders together that way, it also helps me ascertain the relationship between the outreach chair and the other major players in the church, to determine if they're "all on board." We're all familiar with the proverb, "one bad apple spoils the barrel." This dynamic is certainly true in church endeavors. It's for this reason I try to discover going in if there is significant resistance to the mission program we're trying to build.

When I come to a church with the intention of helping the members discover an outreach program that will lead to transformation for individual Christians and the congregation alike, it's because something has led me there. I know that somewhere in that church there's a positive spark of the Spirit. I want to find that spark, affirm it and fan into flame. Therefore, the very worst thing that can happen is for somebody to be behind the scenes constantly pouring water on the fire you're trying to ignite, sabotaging your program. So if there are people who are actively resisting the process, then I want to identify them. Oddly enough, those are the very persons I'm going to try to get on the outreach committee. The best defense is always a good offense. Charge! I want as many people on that committee as I can get. I want them all committed to the specifics of the program that we're going to develop. You might be amazed just how many people are resistant to an idea either because they haven't learned enough about it or because they haven't personally been invited to be part of it.

And as the next step, I'm going to meet with the entire outreach committee. This will be a conversational process as well. There are some things I want to identify with their help and insight. First, I want to hear about their vision for mission. Second, I want to know their level of enthusiasm and hear from them whether or not they think the leadership of the church is committed to mission work.

As I mentioned above, when it comes to serving the Lord through mission work, church members fall into several distinct groups. First, you have that person who says, "I want to go on that mission trip. I want to do that work with my own hands." That's my *volunteer*, as I call him or her. That's the one who comes down, grabs the paintbrush and goes to work.

Then there are *supporters*, those people who enable the physical work of the volunteer. Those who offer support fall into two groups, the first of whom are those who are able to give financial support or provide tangible resources.

For instance, there was a group of young people who came to Westside all the way from Salem, Oregon. It was a long trip. They drove more than thirty hours to get to New Orleans. As I worked with these young people, I noticed they were all mailing out postcards every day. I found out they had held a campaign in their church during the year. Each young person went to individuals in the congregation and said, "I want you to be my partner, my sponsor, to help me go to New Orleans. I will do the labor, but it will be you and me doing mission. I can't do it without your help. And I will report back to you about everything we do." These kids came in every day, wrote a postcard to one of their sponsors that said, "This is what we did today and thank you for sending me."

That's one kind of sponsorship. That was somebody who couldn't get off work or who isn't physically able to come, but wanted to be part of the process. So they wrote a check and sent a kid or an adult.

Then there is the third group, the second kind of supporters—the prayer warriors. I believe deeply in the power of prayer. These are people who cannot volunteer and they may not be able to offer financial support or provide other visible assistance. Still, they are able to pray and in doing support the mission work of their sisters and brothers in Christ. "Righteous prayer availeth much," as the scripture says. Truer words were never spoken. I know that the God Thangs of Westside happened because people—often Christians I have not met and will never meet in this life—prayed for our mission work.

Getting back to developing outreach in your church, I want as many people as possible in the congregation involved in the mission process. Ideally, every member within the congregation is engaged in this outreach program in some way. You either actually go out and physically do the work financially support the work or spiritually support the work through your prayers. My goal is for everyone in the congregation to ask, "What can I do for this mission?" The objective is to involve everybody. Each one of those three groups is necessary and essential. In its own way, each of these three groups is equally important.

That's how we build a mission focus within the church. So how do we go forward then and identify the needs of community? Again, this implies that the congregation has had a preliminary conversation within itself to identify what talents are present within the membership. Below, I'm going to discuss the rather miraculous way in which churches stumble upon ministries for which they are perfectly suited. At this point, let me just make the observation that it does no good to know that Aunt Martha, who lives two streets over from the church, needs brain surgery if you're a carpenter.

Building upon that observation, I hope it goes without saying that we're not just talking about "construction talents" here. I have found that each individual congregation is supplied by the Spirit with members who have different talents, and those talents work together to fulfill the purposes of God for mission.

One church I worked with was really, really into worship—into creative worship experiences. When they recognized this was their passion and talent, at first they were quite frustrated. Their comment to me was, "There's just no way to do outreach when worship is your talent." Not long after that statement was made, they heard about a nearby nursing home that desperately needed people to conduct a worship service. They were asked to come to the home on one Sunday afternoon a month at four o'clock and do a short service and serve communion. They were surprised and delighted and quite enthusiastic.

Soon afterwards, the residents of the home began to insist that worship be held twice a month. Quickly they established an agreement with another church whose members were willing to commit to serving on the other two Sundays and conduct an afternoon service.

One thing that set the Disciples congregation apart in the eyes of the nursing home residents was the celebration of communion. They found that, while a number of other churches were willing to conduct worship there, very few offered communion. Many of the home's residents expressed their gratitude and made comments like, "I haven't had communion in years."

These remarks reminded the volunteers that they needed to take communion to their own homebound church members. This was a case where a church identified its talent, went looking for the corresponding need and was surprised to discover indeed it was out there. Christ was served through their actions. They became much more aware of the needs of others and of how Christ could meet those needs through them. This was a God Thang, and like so many other miracles totally unexpected. Ministering through critical presence doesn't happen only in the Lower Ninth Ward or the Dominican Republic, but also in nursing homes and in the neighborhoods where you live.

Sometimes what your congregation has to offer is not talent but something a lot more tangible. Take for instance the marvelous example of Downey Avenue Christian Church in Indianapolis. There was a fire at Downey Avenue that resulted in the membership having to establish a capital campaign in order to rebuild. It was a true act of walking the extra mile that, while they were raising money for the needs of their own facility, they decided to raise an offering for mission work at Westside as well.

Bob Sieck commented about that by saying:

When we got to the point after our church fire at Downey Avenue Christian Church that we needed to raise funds to rebuild our church, we had already been on several trips to the Gulf Coast to be involved in rebuilding. It seemed like the right thing to do, for our church to commit to raise some funds as part of our capital campaign to do some rehab work in New Orleans.

This is the sort of God Thang that can even emerge out of a disaster—like a church fire. There are no limits to what God might lead your congregation to do through its outreach.

The fact is, it's been one God Thang after another.

Let me get back to the process of establishing the church's mission plan. After I've met with the outreach committee and other interested people, I enlist their help in putting the word out that we're coming to present the plan. We're not meeting with the church board yet. Instead, it's a formative thing, that is, something we want the congregation as a whole to hear, discuss, wrestle with and pray over. As I go into that formation meeting, I explain that we've identified the talents present in the congregation. I also explain that there is an unmet community need over here. Then I ask, how do we bring these two things together? What are the steps to make this happen? What resources do we need? When we ask that question, it's important to realize we're not necessarily talking about money. We're talking about all the whole scope of possible resources. We write down the answers to all these questions and put them in a logical order. This gives the congregation a game plan for action.

I'm often asked as well about whether or not it's necessary to have the official approval of the church board and the congregation before a church enters into a mission project. Concerning board approval, it seems to me so often that a committee within the church will develop a plan on its own. And often during this process the board and the rest of membership comes to be viewed as extraneous. In fact, committees tend to perceive the church board as its bank. Once their plan is derived, the committee goes before the board and says, "Okay, we have this mission plan. We need $2000 to make it happen and we request that the board give us $2000."What I'm saying here is that it's wise for the committee to apprise the board of the mission plan as it's going through this discernment process. If the board is aware of the steps that have been taken, of the deliberation involved, of what the committee has discovered—both about the church and about the needs of the community—it will be watching the process with interest. If the board at least observes the development of the mission plan, there will be less "selling" the idea and more a celebration that a plan has come into being that the board might help bring to fruit. If it's a good plan, asking for the money to implement it gets a lot easier. If the committee can't sell the board on its plan, then either something is wrong with the plan or with the board. In either event, it's important to figure that out as a part of the planning process rather than before the committee is ready to put the plan into action.

I've been asked how I would handle it if the board says, "We don't want to help those people. They aren't like us. There's nothing in it for our church. Traditionally that hasn't been our ministry at all." I think that sort of response probably would have been anticipated based upon that initial meeting with board chair and the pastor when questions about the vision of the church and its leaders were asked. If the congregation's vision was correctly conveyed, it's extremely unlikely that the board would respond by saying it had no desire to support the mission plan.

Suppose, even though you have a real understanding of the board's consensus opinion about the vision, you still face a tremendous amount of resistance. And suppose you're the outreach chair presenting this plan. When you get that negative response, I think you would say to the board, "Here's what I understand about what our congregational vision, that we intend to do A-B-C. Here is the plan the outreach committee put together to honor the church's vision to do A-B-C. So if there's something wrong with the plan, please share it with me. But if there's something wrong with the vision, then we as a board need to look at our vision, and let's deal with it now."

The whole idea of a congregation's vision is paramount. So often in our churches, what is described as the church's "vision" is really the vision of only one or two people. It's not a true, shared vision that the congregation or the board has accepted as its own. This is the very reason I spend so much time stressing the need of discussing and defining the true vision of the church. Many times a church has never intentionally, objectively discussed its shared vision until it enters into a mission process like this. People are often amazed, once they begin to share their ideas about Christian service, just how much of a common vision they share. The other good thing about the congregation as a whole intentionally discussing a shared vision is that it tends to dilute the negativity and influence or those one or two individuals who might disapprove of the mission plan and who actually might be able to derail it despite the intentions of most members and leaders.

In my view, a necessary step in this process is involving the regional minister—and the district or area ministers if the church is within a district or area supported by a minister. My reasoning for this is that these ministers are there to offer the congregation direction, cooperation and support.

Sometimes people want to know why I think it's so important to involve the region. Some folks protest, "We can figure out for ourselves what our talents are and how to use them."

This attitude reminds me of that old adage, "Ready, fire, aim!"

Speaking as a former congregational pastor who is now a regional pastor, I can say with authority that when churches have regional ministers, area ministers, district ministers—whatever you call those of us who do what we do—then those churches really need to take advantage of the resources we offer. Why? Well here are three good reasons. First, it is always good to have the objectivity of a trained professional person who can offer criticism, encouragement and above all honesty. Second, I've often found it to be the case that the folks who don't want to involve regional pastors are also the folks who actively or passively resist the development of the mission planning process. Third, once you as a congregation have made the public statement before someone like a regional minister that your church is going to become involved in a transforming ministry like a real outreach program, it's easier for the church to proceed and harder for the church to back out.

Exactly what resources do regional ministers have to offer a local church that is going through this outreach discernment process? Assuming that we regional pastors are doing our jobs as administrators, at the very least we are aware of what other churches in the region are doing. We can discuss the procedures other churches have used, the progress they have made and the results they are experiencing. We can give advice about the successes and pitfalls other churches have encountered. We can say, "This worked and this didn't. You may face this. You may face that."

I can't overstate how worthwhile it is to have someone with mission experience—perhaps even MMI training—to come into a planning committee to say, "You've got this great idea. You've got these great plans. Let's look together at how do we become accountable to this plan, how can we implement it?"

When should your congregation involve a regional minister? The presence and participation of regional pastors might be a part of an initial dreaming session. Or it may not be utilized until the final planning meeting where the outreach project is being tweaked and firmly established. The important thing is to decide as a church that you are going to involve your region in your mission.

While we're talking about the significance of regional ministers and leaders being involved in the planning process, I'd like to express another thought about the importance of the region and denomination. I cannot stress enough how important it is for a congregation to be cooperative and not try to be a stand-alone church. I think every congregation needs to ask how it's involved at the regional and the denominational level. Ultimately, churches must think of themselves as part of a corporate family. When we plan things as a congregation, we need to ask how we will share what we are doing with our sister churches, with the region and within the denomination. What we are doing locally may have huge importance beyond our own church doors and locality, if for no other reason than sharing the example of Christian service we are setting. Wise individuals know that even the healthiest, smartest strongest person needs other people in her or his life. The same is true of the church. If we had forgotten that, the experience of Westside has taught it to us again. The Westside Mission Center, which has done so much good for so many people, would not have existed, served and thrived if not for the denomination's help and referrals and the wise support of the Great River Region. We are always stronger servants of Christ when we share beyond ourselves.

Whenever your congregation contacts the region to say it's entering into the outreach planning process, it's a prophetic call to the regional ministers. All of us regional pastors must keep before us the reality that the Christian Church (Disciples) is a "ground up" organization, that local churches are autonomous and that we in the regional and denominational offices are called to be resources to our churches who want to be good Christian witnesses through outreach.

In my opinion, it's also important for a congregation going through this process to get a "vote of confidence" from the regional ministers. It signals that the larger church is aware of the mission work you're attempting and supports you in every possible way. In my particular area of the Great River Region when a congregation is entering the mission process, I schedule a Sunday to preach. Depending on what particular church it is and what's appropriate for those circumstances, we make sure we have circulated the news to the congregation through some form of communication exactly what we're thinking about doing. We don't try to give everyone all the details, simply a concise overview. We say something like, "We're working with outreach and we've got some exciting ideas."

Getting back to the process of developing the church's mission plan, after the church leaders, the board, and the congregation have been made aware of what is being discussed, it's time to celebrate the plan in worship. At that point, I go in and preach a sermon that utilizes the Luke 10 passage I've discussed so much: the Good Samaritan Parable, who is my neighbor. We use that to set the basis for discussing who our neighbors are and what the vision of this church is. Then I ask the congregation directly, "What is your vision. This is your church. How do we Christians here live out Christ's command to love our neighbors as we love ourselves?"

What we're trying to accomplish in that presentation, first of all, is educating the congregation. We want people to know that we're going to do some outreach things. Then we want them to reflect about how they might be a part of the mission work. I come back to the "lead, follow or get out of the way" idea. In the process of that message, I say, "I know there are those of you who love to come to church on Sunday morning, to listen to the sermon and then to get up and go home. You're happy with your spiritual life as it is. And that's perfectly acceptable. However there are those of us that within your congregation who feel the need to look around us and ask the question, 'Who is my neighbor,' and do something in response to the answer. And we just want to let you know that we're doing that and it's our intention to involve a large portion of the church family in this mission."

Whenever we make that presentation in worship, our experience has been that a good percentage of members within every congregation immediately express a desire to participate in outreach. Of course, we don't expect everyone in the church to leap up and join in the actual mission work. For each individual who is interested, however, there is definitely a way for that person to be part of the transformational process.

While we're talking about individual responses to the outreach project, I think it's important to mention the pastor's role in all of this. The pastor of the church does not have to be involved in every aspect of the process, but her or his enthusiastic support is essential. Certainly if the pastor is not "on board" with the mission effort, it makes the whole process much more difficult.

I had the experience of working with one church in which the minister was not at all interested in the outreach project. My concern was that he might derail the effort everyone else was putting into the plan. I went to him and said, "I understand that you don't want to do this, but why is it that you don't want to do it? Is it because you don't believe in the program or you don't want to invest the time and effort?"

No pastor is going to say, "I don't believe in being a good neighbor." Rather, a pastor might say, "It's just that I don't want to do it," or "I don't think we have the resources," or something of that nature.

I discussed the matter with the pastor. I asked, "Would you understand if your board said, 'We don't agree with your reluctance. We want to go forward'?" The pastor's answer was, "The board and the congregation can do whatever they want. I'm not going to interfere with the mission."

That was fine with the church leaders. We went back and worked with the board chair and the outreach person and established a real mission program.

In a situation like that, over time one of two things is going to happen. Either the pastor will come to a point of deciding she or he wants to support the outreach program or that church is going to want a new pastor. I also think that the regional pastor can be extremely helpful as a part of the decision making process where there are doubts, confusion, misinformation or reluctance.

I think it's important here to discuss again the distinction between colonial mission and critical presence mission. It all begins with the attitude we have toward assisting people who need our help. Of course, the attitude of the leaders is key, but the attitude of every volunteer is also important. There are those whose attitude is, "If I'm going to help you, I'm going to do it my way. I don't care if you like peas, I'm going to give you carrots. If you don't want to eat my carrots, you can starve to death."

I know it's kind of a radical to say it that way, but I think it expresses my point clearly. Helping everyone involved in your church's outreach work to have the proper attitude is an educational process. Our colonial attitude is innate and insidious; that is, we all have that attitude and it can corrupt our Christian service without our realizing it. Indeed, we don't realize there are many of us who, with varying degrees of certainty, are convinced we know what's best for the people we want to help. Our attitude is, "You know, I have no desire to help these folks if they aren't going to get what I'm trying to do and if they aren't going to show some gratitude."

I think we have to take a step back from that attitude. We have to say to ourselves, "Now wait a minute. Whose resources are we really using while we are trying to help others?"

I think if we are honest, we can look at any disadvantaged person we might end up working with and say, "There but for the grace of God go I."

Regardless of your station in life, if you are considering reaching out to help other people and you can't see God's hand at work in your own affluence—great or small as it may be—and you can't see God's hand at work providing your good life, then you need to enter into a time of spiritual growth. I think we all need to recognize that it's "our Father," it's not just "my Father".

If there is a pivotal role that church pastors and regional pastors play in educating us for outreach work, it is in addressing our attitudes. It is instilling in us an awareness of the distinction between colonialism and critical presence. It is in encouraging us to grow spiritually so that we can grow in mission.

When I come in to the church to present on the idea of critical presence and I ask, "Who is my neighbor," many in the congregation understand that this presentation is building upon the prior meetings we have had. They know there is a movement to involve the membership in outreach work. So when I get to that point, I make a blanket statement about who is and isn't eligible to participate in mission work and how they can help.

I say, "I know what some of you are thinking right now. Some of you are thinking, 'I'm too young to do mission.' I've had children, with their parents of course, as young as five working on a mission trip. I know some of you are going to say, 'I'm too old to do mission.' And I've had a couple in their nineties doing mission. So those of you who fit somewhere between five and ninety-two, let me assure you that if you want to, you *can* do mission.

"Having said that, let me point out that there are three different mission groups into which you might fit. There are those who are going to go and physically do this work. There are the people who will help support this work with their resources. And there are the people who are not physically able to do the work and may not have the resources to help. They will be our prayer warriors and they'll support the mission that way. There's also a fourth group. It's made up of folks who honestly enjoy coming to church but just don't get into doing outreach. I'm comfortable with whichever one of those groups you're in."

Having established these distinctions for the church members, then I tell the story of the missional church. I express the reality that, if we are going to grow as Christians and as a congregation, we must through our actions positively, affirmatively live out the answer to the question, "Who is my neighbor?" We must decide who in our community are our neighbors in need of the help we can offer. We must decide what we're going to do about addressing those needs.

Karen Zuver writes about her experience in first hearing the story of the missional church when I came to Hiram, Ohio, to present on the needs we were facing in New Orleans and asking people to come to Westside and help:

> *How do you get involved in a cause that's the size and depth of the destruction that a little wind called 'Katrina' caused? You go to a fundraising dinner that area churches are putting on to hear a man you've never heard of talk about his love for an area of your country. But, hey, the food will be great. And maybe you'll put a little money in the coffer.*
>
> *Then this wonderful voice begins to speak. He talks about NOLA with such a conviction and passion that it mesmerizes you to listen. It connects with something deep in your soul. You turn to your son, who is really on there for the food, and there on his face is the same look you know is on your own. You realize then you must make the sacrifice and go.*

Believe me, I know that this implies sacrifice and commitment. I know it implies getting out of our little comfort zones. Not long ago someone brought me a funny sign to hang on the wall. It mirrors perfectly what goes on inside us when we think about giving ourselves for this ministry. Each month of the year is listed on the sign that says something like this:

"We can't do this because it's January and we're trying to pay off the Christmas bills. We can't do this because it's February and it's too cold. We can't do this because it's March and pollen's in the air and I'm allergic. We can't do this because it's April and I haven't figured up my taxes. . . ."

Of course, you don't have to look very far or hard to find something every day, every week and every month to give you a reason not to enter into mission work. And I can appreciate there are people whose priorities or their workload will be the reason they say they can't do outreach. That's not for me to judge. I must say, however, that our example of service and sacrifice is Jesus Christ, who stood up and he opened his arms as wide as he could. They drove nails in his hands and as they were doing it, he said, "I love you this much."

It is in light of his example that we must each make our own decision about what we're going to do. You know that place in the Bible when Jesus says, "You don't know the hour or the day?" What if it's today— not the Judgment Day for you, but rather the day of opportunity to minister to someone else? What if your faithful service could reach one soul that has not said "yes" to Christ and today's their day?

Whatever happened to Vance's wake up bell?

All in all, how long does the process of becoming a mission church take? Well, it might be years in the planning before its put into action, or it might develop as suddenly as stormy weather. And in fact it might be a little of both.

Tom Sikes had been prophetic about the need for his congregation to be intentionally missional for a number of years. Then suddenly the day came when the church was indeed called by the Lord to reach out. He made these comments about the experience:

For four years from 2001-2005, I had preached and encouraged our church to use the Missional Church model that invites members to see themselves as missionaries at home, at work and beyond. Using the model of Acts 8:26-40, God calls us to "get up and go on the wilderness road south at high noon between Jerusalem and Gaza." This is our call today. So on the last day of August 2005, we had the option to get up and go to the coast and help those who were affected by Katrina or stay put. The church chose to get up and go!

Led by Dr. Randy Nance with a host of medical support staff and volunteers, we boarded RV's, cars and trucks and headed south on the "wilderness road" from Meridian to the Mississippi Gulf Coast. We went to "ground zero" and saw the need with our own eyes.

We were called to open a medical clinic in Moss Point, Mississippi, at the African-American church there. This little church was not flooded like most of that city. For some reason it was just high enough. So the pastor opened the church as a mission. We poured in there with many teams and equipment and even put a trailer to better serve the people for the duration of recovery.

Dr. Nance and I slept outside at night and reflected on the mission. He modeled what happened to Philip in Acts 8. He indeed felt the call to "get up and go" and not worry about insurance and liability. He went and served with all his heart alongside his family and staff. Very few doctors came to help. But he did. And he is to be commended.

Ironically, after this he formed a new company to provide modular homes for survivors called New Gulf Homes. We helped him in the initial stages of forming this company and assisting in the navigation through the politics of the Gulf Coast, seeking support and approval for modular housing to serve any in need.

I'd like to address a question I'm often asked: "How do we go about getting the word out into the community that we are engaged in real mission? How do we discover who might need our help?"

There are two aspects to this. First, it's been my experience that once you start doing some community action things the word spreads itself very quickly. Once you go over and fix Aunt Martha's screen door, it won't be long before somebody else down the street turns up on your doorstep to tell you that he or she also has a screen door that needs fixing. So word of mouth is one side of it.

Second, almost every newspaper in every town—especially the small towns—is desperately interested in local news stories, human interest stories. This is good advertising and it doesn't cost. There are Kiwanis Clubs, Sertoma Clubs, Jaycees—you name it. These service organizations are, by the way, wonderful opportunities for your pastor to go and speak. They present a wonderful opportunity for your outreach chair to speak, or for any individual in the church who is gifted as a speaker. Don't hesitate to involve your regional pastor in this. Whenever she or he is available, that person should be ready to speak on the importance of outreach and the concept of critical presence, which is such a foreign idea to so many people. Schedule these leaders in for a luncheon at one of these service organizations and let them speak.

There is a multitude of ways to tell the story of what you're doing in your community: TV, radio, local government, or any public venue that gives you the opportunity to share. I've become more and more aware that the internet has opened up a treasure chest of new ways to promote the outreach ministries of our churches: electronic bulletin boards, blogs, Twitter or Facebook. There are all kind of places on the internet where information, reports and requests can be posted for free.

It's important as well to be open to the participation of non-members or non-participating members in the church's outreach. We have a tendency to say, "We're the church and this is what we're doing," without realizing that we're being insular and exclusive. It's important to realize when we're doing mission that we have the opportunity—the necessity—to be inclusive.

I had people come to Westside on mission trip and say to me, "We don't go to church on a regular basis, but we heard about this mission trip and we want to go do something good for Jesus."

On more than one occasion, I had people say, "I

ain't going to church. But I believe in God. I believe in Jesus. And I want to do something." I understand they are asking me to involve them in helping their neighbors.

While we're talking about being open, we should consider involving other congregations in our work. I think we should start with other churches of our denomination. After all, the Campbell-Stone movement began with groups of churches doing ministry and sharing the Gospel cooperatively. Outreach ministry, as we learned in the aftermath of Katrina and through Westside Mission Center, is at its core and by its very nature ecumenical.

Non-profit organizations in the community that are interested in outreach, for example the Salvation Army, might also be interested in the mission work your church is doing, as well as helpful non-governmental agencies (NGO's) that may be searching for ways to work in your community. A good example of this comes to mind. When I was working with homeless folk in Little Rock, I met a sergeant of the Salvation Army. He and his wife never got any time off. I volunteered to go down and preach for him one Sunday night just to give him a night off. After that, he began to work with me in our outreach.

I think we also should be open to seeking the support of our elected officials. Depending on what your mission is, you might want to go to your mayor or to your councilperson and say, "You are our representative and our leader and we need your endorsement." The city or county or state may have resources suited to the mission project your church is trying to organize and your elected representatives may be the key to helping secure those things necessary to achieve your outreach goals.

It's important to recognize that these outreach projects we're talking about are local. It's not necessary for your congregation to travel great distances to find people who have needs you can address. I believe with everything in me that so many of us will drive all the way to New Orleans, Louisiana, to do mission and all the while not realize there is unmet need just around the corner. Don't get me wrong—volunteers are still needed to go to the Gulf Coast. That's a real need that hits close to home for us in the Great River Region. Still, if Westside were active today, I think I would tell our Westside volunteers to be aware that, on the way out of your town as you travel to New Orleans, you'll be driving by someone who really needs your help. It's worthwhile to identify that need and to examine the talents we have that will allow us to address it.

While we're talking about reaching out to the community, I think it's important to establish some principles for what we do and how we do it. We have to establish some boundaries for helping, to realize there is a difference between a "hand up" and a "hand out." There has to be a balance as we live out Jesus' command to Peter, "Feed my sheep." Clearly, there is a great deal of need in the world today. Christ excluded no one from his love and thus I don't intend to exclude anyone. Still, my discernment is that we should not allow people to take advantage of us.

One important recognition, I believe, is that there are limitations. There are only so many resources out there with which we can help folks. My intention is to work first with those in need who have no place else to turn for help. So when someone comes to me to ask for assistance, I want to be able to ascertain whether or not that person has other available resources. If someone does have access to other help, I want to point out to that person what resources they already have. There are times when critical presence is lived out by helping someone recognize resources outside our mission. In doing so, I preserve what limited goods I have at my disposal for others.

For instance, if someone comes to me wanting a meal and I know that all they have to do is walk across the street to St. Luke's for a free lunch, I'm going to walk with them and show them where they can eat. In doing so, I've avoided needlessly duplicating the outreach ministry of others. I've also preserved food or funds that I can give to someone who is not able to get to St. Luke's. That's one side of it, the side that deals with what we have to offer to others.

The other side of it has to do with learning how to minister to people in need, which is certainly not as easy as one might think. To use our Lord's analogy from the Sermon on the Mount, when I've been "struck on one cheek," it takes an awful lot to be willing to turn the other cheek. Please allow me to confess my humanness here: much as I wish I had, I just have not arrived at that pure spiritual place yet. If you strike me on one cheek, I'm going to step back. I don't want you hitting me. If I can't come around you without your trying to strike me, I'm going to avoid you altogether.

Sometimes the people we most want to avoid are the ones who most need our help. Sometimes the people who need our help the most are also the most difficult to assist. Some of us have found it transforming in a positive way to minister to those who take what we have to offer without gratitude, without it making a real spiritual difference in them. Not everyone you help will be appreciative of your effort and provision, but there is still value in helping—if you can. It takes deep faith, patience and thick skin to be able to minister in that way.

Sometimes, however, you may not be able to bring yourself to assist those who are manipulative, abusive, dishonest or filled with an attitude of "enraged entitlement." If you find you cannot minister to such folks without losing your integrity and dignity as a Christian, I hope you'll be forgiving enough of yourself to refer those individuals to other missions and agencies—where possible—and then move on to find others in need whom you can assist. Our Lord was speaking the prophetic truth when he said, "The poor are with you always." There are many people in your community who need your assistance and who are ready for the ministry of critical presence. They will do what they can do to be a part of the process. These are the people with whom it is easiest to work. And it is in working with them that the transforming power of the living Christ is most clearly experienced.

Of course, when I ask the famous question, "Who is my neighbor," it seems to imply that I must never turn down anyone I can help who is gravely in need of assistance. Over the years, I've discovered that helping people requires a great deal of wisdom and sometimes even the courage to say, "This is how much I'm willing to do and I won't help beyond this." Some good-hearted volunteers and people in your church may not be able to take that stand. This can end up being a problem for them and for their church, as well as creating an issue for the people they are trying to assist by not establishing clear limits.

One example comes to mind quite clearly. When Jeannie and I were in Benton, Arkansas, we started a little program called YANA that was meant to help homeless people. We started it because I had gotten very, very frustrated with a certain religious group in Little Rock. This group would give a homeless man a meal, but only if he was willing to sit and listen to a sermon before he ate. I believe in carrying the message, but I don't think that's the way you do it. That's forced evangelism, which I recognize now is a form of colonialism.

Jeannie and I decided to go a different route. We made up some little bags, little packets with food in them. There was enough food in one of them to last a fellow for a day or so. We put a map in there that showed how to get to the mission. Then we would just go out and if we saw a homeless person on the side of the road, we would stop. I would get out and just ask, "Would you like something to eat?"

Obviously these men were by in large very skeptical. Their doubts diminished, however, when I gave them some food and asked nothing in return. Before long, we became known around the Little Rock area for this ministry.

Some of the church members came to me and said, "We want to do this as well." So I taught them how to go about it.

Eventually, however, I began to notice that some of our members, who out of the goodness of their hearts wanted so desperately to help, were being taken advantage of by some of street folks who knew how to "play the game". There was one particular volunteer, a woman with a strong personality—in fact, she was a cable splicer for the phone company, a physical person who worked outdoors, but someone with a very tender heart—who came to me. She shared that one particular homeless person had gotten into her pocket for hundreds of dollars.

She said, "I don't know how to say 'no' because

that's my neighbor." Obviously, there's a point when you have to decide how much of a hand up a person needs. Sacrificial giving—of money, time or talent—doesn't imply foolish giving. One of my clearest observations about serving Christ is that serving people at the moment of critical presence never leaves a feeling of regret. It's empowering and transforming. You never wish you hadn't given so much of yourself.

Let me go back for a moment to the notion of vision. My vision of the YANA program was to feed somebody for a day, but to put them in the position where, if they so desired, they could be "taught to fish" so they could feed themselves. It was not our intention to pick them up off the street and give them a place to live, and money to spend and new clothes. That was not my mission. My mission was to give them a hand up. I did not see that food packet as a hand out but a hand up.

Turning once again to the outreach ministry your church is developing. Let's assume that we've followed the process just as we'd laid it out in this chapter. Let's suppose that your congregation has done a good job of discovering unmet local needs and begins to do outreach within its own community. I predict that transformation will occur within your members, within the congregation itself and within the individuals to whom you are reaching out. That's still not the end of process. There are a couple of responses, I believe, we must make as a congregation as we are moving forward in mission.

First, I cannot overstate how important it is for congregations to share the news about their mission work with other churches. As the scripture says, "As cool water is to a thirsty soul, so is good news from a far country." When we hear of a creative outreach project that really helps people, it's refreshing to all of us in the extended church family. To be sure, there is probably someone in your congregation whose talent is being able to disseminate news to the area, region and denomination.

Second, a congregation must not forget to maintain and reinforce its regional and denominational connections as well. Within our denomination—and my sense is this is true within the world of Protestant churches—there is a disconnect that exists particularly between small churches with the rest of the denomination. I've seen this, for instance, in regard to our General Assembly. There might be a controversial, hotly debated resolution, but the grassroots people in small congregations often don't know what's going on. They neither have a firm grasp on the issue nor any conception of how it might apply to them.

Dealing with that "distance" between congregations and the denomination is certainly beyond the scope of this book, but I'm convinced that one solution to the disconnect is to involve congregations of every size in outreach work. *Reaching out to people in need is a great equalizer.* If the members of small congregations in small towns are given the opportunity in the right way to participate in the world of larger mission, my sense is that they not only can but they will. The alternative can be so disheartening. So often, we see small congregations that used to participate in world mission. Then they just participated in national mission. Then they just participated in regional mission. Finally the day comes where they no longer participates in local mission or any mission at all.

Outreach is much like a spiritual muscle. If we don't exercise it, it will atrophy and become useless to us. As Protestants and Disciples, we have largely quit doing the things that made us as the force in America that we were. It's our own fault. I intend that to be one of the essential messages conveyed in this book: we've stopped doing the mission work that defined us and we must return to that. Look at what Jesus modeled for us. Remember the Parable of the Good Samaritan and what he told the lawyer at the end of the dialogue between them, "Go and do. Go and do." Nowhere did he say, "Sit on your rear and watch." He said, "Go and do."

Everyone who knows Vance agrees, he gets right to the heart of the matter, even if he has to go right through the wall to do it!

Suppose, though, that we succeed in stirring our congregations—large and small, growing and dying—to become engaged in outreach. There's something that is so exciting and dynamic to think about. As the mission of each church grows, we will have a powerful story to tell to the whole region. My vision is that, anything we do—positive or negative—is contagious. If we don't quit putting out fires and begin to start some fires, I believe we're going to die—as congregations and as a denomination.

A big part of the problem is that First Christian Church in your town has no idea what Central Christian Church in my town is doing. I believe each of those churches has a great deal going on that would be intriguing, inspiring and motivating to its sister churches. It's hugely important for those churches to get reacquainted with one another, if for no other reason than the opportunity for each to broaden its perspective and broaden its outlook on what can be done to serve God.

There are, of course, many other benefits that can come from this type of networking: a depth of spirituality, a depth of the sense of spiritual family and everything from denominational growth to congregational growth. Here's a really crazy thing, a great irony: *if we quit focusing on church growth and start focusing on the things Christ told us to do, the church will grow.*

I recognize that there are some folks who are so skeptical that they want nothing to do with the General Offices. This is a difficult issue for me and a difficult issue for us as a church, whether we're talking about the local church, the regional church or the general church. How can we deal with the reluctance?

The answer I think to that is very clear. The skeptic I'm describing is a spiritual person. If you are a spiritual person, you have a living relationship with Jesus Christ. If you have a living relationship with Jesus Christ, then it seems to me to be essential to involve our Savior in this issue. I think we need to pray, "Lord, here is a concern I have and I don't know what you want me to do." Then the skeptical person should express the doubts and difficulties he or she has and say, "Lord, I need you to guide me. Show me what you want me to do."

My personal experience has been that every time I have ever approached Christ in prayer with the right attitude, the Lord has never failed to tell me what to do, to give me the direction I needed when I needed it. The attitude I'm describing is, "Lord I'm open to what you going to say to me and I'm willing to do what you're going to tell me to do."

I may not always receive the answer to prayer that I wanted to hear. In fact, there have been times I've had to bite my tongue a little bit. When I'm really willing to listen to the Lord, the answers I receive are always dependable and always reflective of God's will. I'm committed to doing what the Lord wants me to do in my own life.

I want to take that a nickel further and say that I have the utmost faith in the majority of the people in the church with whom I have worked. Their hearts are in the right place. They've got the "want to." Sometimes we as leaders and we as brothers and sisters in Christ have to impact that a little bit, direct it a little bit, focus it a little bit. Sometimes we just have to calm our hearts and pray about it. If we as a people will get on our knees—literally or figuratively—and go back to God and recommit ourselves to finding and following God's will, we will recover true direction and rebuild fellowship with one another in ways that are desperately needed today.

This is precisely what happened as Disciples along the Gulf Coast pulled together in the aftermath of Katrina. Michael Elmore described it this way:

In the midst of all this, people have come together. For Disciples churches down here, it has been a great experience to be connected with other Disciples across our denomination. Before Katrina, we often felt unconnected with the larger church. Volunteers have come and given us hope that we are not alone. Many of us also came to see that the answer to our problems is not in the government—local, state or national—but in neighbors reaching out to help.

Local congregations have taken on new life as they found a purpose beyond themselves. Many of the congregations I work with were struggling to survive, uncertain of their future and of their mission and purpose for being. They became "church" again. They remembered who they were and their lives were transformed. They connected with other Disciples around our denomination and learned about their hopes and struggles and discovered they were not alone. They felt cared for.

For volunteers, I think the same was true. They moved outside the walls and outside themselves and their worlds and discovered God at work in the midst of disaster and thus remembered who they were and why they were. They became an incarnational presence. We saw God in their faces and they saw God in the faces of those to whom they were reaching out and we were all changed. It has been a truly beautiful experience in the midst of all the disaster.

I also believe it's very important to bring people

together from diverse backgrounds, whether it be ethnic, gender, age or regional differences. One of my favorite sayings is, "You have the choice to be a big fish in a little pond, or you can get out in the ocean and swim and become the fish that God wants you to be." If we decide to remain just in our little pond, we lose the vast resources of the ocean, resources intended to help us grow. If we take the leap of faith and get out in the deep water, we will grow immeasurably more than we ever could in the small pond. I don't necessarily know the best way to express that, but I have certainly learned how to live it.

The experience of watching others do mission and ministry can tremendously empowering. It's that exposure to other ideas that makes us grow as a people. How many times have we seen somebody do something and say, "I can do that! I thought about trying it once, but I didn't do it. Now I see it being done and I know I can do it."

Tom Russell wrote of his surprise at seeing loved ones rediscovering one another in a new light as they were working side-by-side in mission:

When married couples share in mission they share a new and renewed special relationship that—even though I have experienced it—I don't quite know how to put into words. My relationship with my own brother was renewed when I saw God's presence at work in him. He saved a trailer that was about to be taken to the dump. He brought it to Westside in 2007. After some rather major rebuilding at the hands of the youth group of the Howard Avenue Christian Church, it began to be used. Westside eventually donated it to Pastor Howard

Washington, who still uses it almost daily to help get materials to jobs for volunteers to use in the rebuilding effort. It is all part of a God Thang!

Suppose we consider how this reaching out to other churches might work on an even larger scale. Let's say that within each congregation we have three groups of people. We have the youth. We have the adults. We have the older adults.

At this point, I'd like to say I think it's an important thing for the older adults to mentor the young people in their churches. The older folks have knowledge about mission work that younger people need to learn. The younger ones have the enthusiasm that comes with youth. If we start a mentoring program, it should follow the youth throughout the mission learning experience—all the way from their neighborhoods through to global mission stage. This sort of inclusivity, older adults working with young people, can be a tremendous building block for all types of growth within the congregation as well.

Specifically with the youth, as we talk about the expansion of our mission awareness from next door to state to regional to national and then to international, I envision us starting our young people off working on outreach in the local community. In this way we can give them a sense of what mission is about without great expense and without inadvertently creating in them the attitude that you have to go somewhere else to help people in need. Then we take them somewhere in their home state. They get to spend the night out—which is the fun part of it. Then we bring them to mission site like Westside, where there was a great natural disaster and there is still tremendous need. At some point, however—and it's almost like I envision this to be a "senior trip" the young people might take with their church families—we have them visit a developing nation like Haiti, the Dominican Republic, Guatemala or Mexico for instance. There is literally nothing else that will broaden their experience in this way. It is invaluable for young people to "see how the rest of the world lives."

An experience like that also has a great ability to drive home truths and lessons learned from the Bible. As Jesus said in Matthew and in Luke, a tree is known by its fruit. When we give young people the opportunity to see lots of different environments, they will have a fuller understanding of what's meaningful and worthy in their own. They'll also acquire the ability to "get outside of themselves." It's important, I think to introduce them to the mother who is living in a shanty with a dirt floor and her children are on that floor with their schoolbooks open doing their homework (which, incidentally, they know is not an option but mandatory). I think they will learn a lot about what is truly meaningful, virtuous and enduring—in contrast to the ephemeral, fashionable qualities promoted by the popular culture with which young people are continually inundated. Those experiences will say more to our youth than a thousand sermons could say.

It's important to note that the sort of needs assessment we do within our local communities to locate needs we can address with the talents present in our churches is also a dynamic that works on a global scale as well. However, it requires a "reality check", because things are done different in different nations and cultures. Part of avoiding a colonial attitude, I've learned, is being aware of the uniqueness of each specific place where we do outreach.

When I was first sent to the Dominican Republic, my sense was that we were going to go over and we were going to build houses, schools or hospitals. I thought that, because I had the mission and construction experience, I was going to be asked to build something. To be candid I even had people already calling me saying, "I have materials. I have metal building manufacturing facilities. I will furnish you a building to erect." Only when I got to the Dominican Republic, I found out eventually that they don't use metal buildings over there. They use buildings made with concrete blocks.

If I had approached the trip from a critical presence viewpoint, I would have strived first to find out from the Dominicans' perspective what was the greatest need that I had the ability to meet. I should have asked, is there a building that needs to be constructed? Is it proper for us to build it? What can I do to address the concerns and needs of the people I was called to assist?

For instance, while I was there in the Dominican Republic, we learned that Sister Denise needed a new building for her *Caminante* ministry. It was going to be made of concrete blocks. I listened to Sister Denise and discovered there were some folks over there, Dominican nationals, who were making just the sort of blocks we needed. It was a start up and they desperately need customers. They were making these blocks out in the countryside.

This is an aspect of mission assessment that is true locally or globally. It's really a part of matching the talents of the volunteers with the needs of the people they are assisting. It requires a basic understanding of the idea of critical presence.

Just as an aside to that, what we identified when we

finally got over there is that there are forty evangelical churches in the Dominican Republic each of whom needs a sister church in the United States. So we are in the process now of formulating a plan where we take the 120 churches from the Great River Region and match them up with the Dominican churches. In this way, two or three churches over here will have sister churches over there. Once we get to that point, we sit down—our three churches, their one church—and say, "What is God saying to us? How can we work together to address needs in the most appropriate, helpful way?" When we proceed in this way, we open lots of doors for the Spirit to come in, we set the stage to experience lots of God Thangs.

I'd like to close by sharing a children's sermon I heard not long ago. It was given by a woman who is a lay member of one of the churches I serve. She called the children forward and proceeded to teach them an unforgettable lesson about prayer. She had them kneel in front of the chancel, put their hands together and repeat after her: "Dear Lord, I love you. I know you love me. I promise to obey you. Thank you, Father. Amen."

After that, I got up to preach and I said the congregation, "This is not in my notes, but it really needs to be said because it's so important."

Then I had the congregation do the same thing the children did. We bowed our heads and they repeated that simple prayer: "Dear Lord, I love you. I know you love me. I promise to obey you. Thank you, Father. Amen."

And then I said to them, "I have a sermon that is prepared to deliver to you, but if I preach for the rest of this day, I cannot bring a better message than the one that was just taken to the children."

I think all of us who accepted Christ accepted his lordship. When our Savior was asked, what is the greatest commandment, he said, "Love God with all your heart, your soul, your strength and your mind. And love your neighbor as you love yourself." If we rise each day and say that simple prayer, I believe it will lead us to expressing our love for God by expressing our love for our neighbors. I believe the Lord will show us how we can love our neighbors by helping them at the moment of critical presence. I know that loving our neighbors at the moment of critical presence will transform them and us. As a result, I know we will all be renewed as we experience the presence of God.

This farewell to the Lower Ninth Ward was quite prophetic, as volunteers and churches regularly returned.

Those seeking congregational or individual consultation regarding Critical Presence, the Missional Church and utilizing outreach ministry for congregational revitalization may contact the author as listed below:

Bro. Vance Moore
9139 Tank Rd.
Crystal Springs, MS 39059

601-506-0882

Email: BroVance@grrcc.org

Addendum

An Overview of the Critical Presence Plan
For Outreach and Congregational Revitalization

A. The Outreach Committee

    a. Contact the Board Chair/Pastor; identify the Outreach Committee

    b. Evaluate the Outreach Chair's strengths and weaknesses

    c. Acquire the names and contact information for all committee members

    d. Initial Meeting Agenda

        i. Seek the help/blessing/guidance of God

        ii. Ask the question, what is our goal/why do we exist as a church?

            1. What is the role of the youth?

            2. What is the role of our adults?

            3. What is the role of our seniors?

iii.Who else in the church needs to be
on this committee?

iv.Identify our talents/gifts

1.Who will be our
volunteers?

2.Who will be our sponsors?

3.Who will be our
supporters?

v.Identify the needs in our
community

1.Discuss the distinction
between "hand up" and
"hand out"

vi.Draft an initial plan to "Fill the
Need"

vii.Set a date to bring an initial draft
of the plan to the Regional
Minister and Church Board

B.The Church Board

a.Present the "Fill the Need" plan to the
Church Board

b.Identify the support/issues;
resolve/consensus

c.Seek a vote of support

d.Ask, how do we communicate our outreach plan to the whole church?

C.The Pastor

a.Discuss the Church Board resolution

b.Discuss ideas for presenting to the church

c.Seek commitment to support/participate

d.Determine the Pastor's role in educating the church about the "Missional Critical Presence" role of the church

e.Plan for a visit from the Regional Pastor—preaching about Critical Presence

D.The Church

a.Present the Church Board's report to the church

i.How do we communicate so the entire church can be aware of our plans?

ii.Identify members who are ready to volunteer

iii.Identify resources

1.Do, go, send, sponsor

E.The Community

a.Awareness

i.How do we get the word out?

        1.Public announcements (no cost)

        2.Bulletin boards

    b.Involvement

        i.Encourage non-members to participate

        ii.Share the plan with the interfaith community

        iii.Share the plan with non-profit organizations

    c.Commitment

        i.Community leaders

        ii.Interfaith community

        iii.Non-profit organizations

F.Next Door

    a.How to locate "needs" in this community

    b.How to locate "resources" in this community

G.Down the Road

    a.Connecting with the region

        i.Awareness of the need/opportunity to serve

        ii.Possible resources

    b.Your church connection

i.Identify talent

ii.Identify resources

H.Into the World

    a.Region/Global Missions Partnership

        i.Global community needs assessment

        ii.Match church to mission

    b.Your church connection

        i.Match talent to need

        ii.Identify resources

Bro. Vance Moore

Photo Credits

We are thankful for all our volunteers who shared their photographs. In particular, thanks to the churches and photographers listed below.

Vance Moore

First Christian Church, Winston-Salem, NC, p. 9
Westside Christian Church, Algiers, Louisiana, p. 11
Westside Christian Church, Algiers, Louisiana, p. 13
The Kentucky Six, p. 16
Lindsey Gillespie, p. 19
Mike Lindsay p. 26
First Christian Church, Winston-Salem, NC, p. 30
Wes Brooks, p. 31
Mike Lindsay, p. 33
First Christian Church, Meridian, Mississippi, p. 39
Westside Christian Church, Algiers, Louisiana, p. 41
Westside Christian Church, Algiers, Louisiana, p. 48
Westside Christian Church, Algiers, Louisiana, p. 59
Westside Christian Church, Algiers, Louisiana, p. 64
Lindsey Gillespie, p. 69
Westside Christian Church, Algiers, Louisiana, p. 72
First Christian Church, Winston-Salem, NC, p. 75
Westside Christian Church, Algiers, Louisiana, p. 77
Wes Brooks, p. 79
Wes Brooks, p. 82
Lindsey Gillespie, p. 90
First Christian Church, Winston-Salem, NC, p. 92
First Christian Church, Winston-Salem, NC, p. 99
Mike Lindsay, p. 101
Mike Lindsay, p. 106
Westside Christian Church, Algiers, Louisiana, p. 107
Westside Christian Church, Algiers, Louisiana, p. 113
Janice West Taylor, p. 115
Westside Christian Church, Algiers, Louisiana, p. 120
First Christian Church, Meridian, Mississippi, p. 123
Wes Brooks, p. 125
First Christian Church, Winston-Salem, NC, p. 128

202

Mike Lindsay, p. 129
Lindsey Gillespie, p. 134
Westside Christian Church, Algiers, Louisiana, p. 140
Lindsey Gillespie, p. 147
Lindsey Gillespie, p. 163
Lindsey Gillespie, p. 175
Mike Lindsay, p. 186
First Christian Church, Winston-Salem, NC, p. 195
Lindsey Gillespie, Front Cover Photo
Westside Christian Church, Back Cover Photo